BOOKS FROM THE GET 800 COLLECTION
FOR COLLEGE BOUND STUDENTS

28 SAT Math Lessons to Improve Your Score in One Month
    Beginner Course
    Intermediate Course
    Advanced Course
New SAT Math Problems arranged by Topic and Difficulty Level
320 SAT Math Problems arranged by Topic and Difficulty Level
500 SAT Math Problems arranged by Topic and Difficulty Level
SAT Verbal Prep Book for Reading and Writing Mastery
320 SAT Math Subject Test Problems
    Level 1 Test
    Level 2 Test
320 SAT Chemistry Subject Test Problems
Vocabulary Builder
28 ACT Math Lessons to Improve Your Score in One Month
    Beginner Course
    Intermediate Course
    Advanced Course
320 ACT Math Problems arranged by Topic and Difficulty Level
320 GRE Math Problems arranged by Topic and Difficulty Level
320 AP Calculus AB Problems
320 AP Calculus BC Problems
Physics Mastery for Advanced High School Students
400 SAT Physics Subject Test and AP Physics Problems
SHSAT Verbal Prep Book to Improve Your Score in Two Months
555 Math IQ Questions for Middle School Students
555 Advanced Math Problems for Middle School Students
555 Geometry Problems for High School Students
Algebra Handbook for Gifted Middle School Students
1000 Logic and Reasoning Questions for Gifted and Talented
    Elementary School Students

CONNECT WITH DR. STEVE WARNER

www.facebook.com/SATPrepGet800

www.youtube.com/TheSATMathPrep

www.twitter.com/SATPrepGet800

www.linkedin.com/in/DrSteveWarner

www.pinterest.com/SATPrepGet800

plus.google.com/+SteveWarnerPhD

500 New SAT Math Problems arranged by Topic and Difficulty Level

For the Revised SAT March 2016 and Beyond

Dr. Steve Warner

1. Purchase a TI-84 or equivalent calculator

It is recommended that you use a TI-84 or comparable calculator for the SAT. Answer explanations in this book will always assume you are using such a calculator.

2. Take a practice SAT to get your preliminary SAT math score

You can use the Get 800 Diagnostic Math Test beginning on page 13, your last PSAT/SAT math score, or an official College Board practice SAT for this. Use this score to help you determine the problems you should be focusing on (see page 8 for details).

3. Claim your FREE bonuses

See page 199 for a link that will give you access to solutions to all the supplemental problems in this book and solutions to the Diagnostic Test.

4. 'Like' my Facebook page

This page is updated regularly with SAT prep advice, tips, tricks, strategies, and practice problems. Visit the following webpage and click the 'like' button.

www.facebook.com/SATPrepGet800

INTRODUCTION
THE PROPER WAY TO PREPARE

There are many ways that a student can prepare for the SAT. But not all preparation is created equal. I always teach my students the methods that will give them the maximum result with the minimum amount of effort.

The book you are about to read is self-contained. Each problem was carefully created to ensure that you are making the most effective use of your time while preparing for the SAT. By grouping the problems given here by level and topic I have ensured that you can focus on the types of problems that will be most effective to improving your score.

There are two math sections on the SAT: one where a calculator is allowed and one where it is not. I therefore recommend trying to solve as many problems as possible both with and without a calculator. If a calculator is required for a specific problem, it will be marked with an asterisk (*).

Note: "Problem Solving" questions appear only on the calculator section. So, if you wish, you can allow yourself to always use a calculator for these questions. However, it's never a bad idea to practice without a calculator whenever it is possible to do so. Once again, any problem that is not marked with an asterisk (*) does not need a calculator to be solved.

1. Using this book effectively

- Begin studying at least three months before the SAT.
- Practice SAT math problems for ten to twenty minutes each day.
- Choose a consistent study time and location.

You will retain much more of what you study if you study in short bursts rather than if you try to tackle everything at once. So, try to choose about a twenty-minute block of time that you will dedicate to SAT math each day. Make it a habit. The results are well worth this small time commitment.

- Every time you get a question wrong, **mark it off, no matter what your mistake**.
- Begin each study session by first redoing problems from previous study sessions that you have marked off.
- If you get a problem wrong again, **keep it marked off**.

Note that this book often emphasizes solving each problem in more than one way. Please listen to this advice. The same question is not generally repeated on any SAT, so the important thing is for you to learn as many techniques as possible.

Being able to solve any specific problem is of minimal importance. The more methods you have to solve a single problem the more prepared you will be to tackle a problem you have never seen before, and the quicker you will be able to solve that problem. Also, if you have multiple methods for solving a single problem, then on the actual SAT when you "check over" your work you will be able to redo each problem in a different way. This will eliminate all "careless" errors on the actual exam. Note that in this book the quickest solution to any problem will always be marked with an asterisk (*).

Practice problems of the appropriate level: Roughly speaking about one third of the math problems on the SAT are easy, one third are medium, and one third are hard. If you answer two thirds of the math questions on the SAT correctly, then your score will be approximately a 600 (out of 800). That's right—you can get about a 600 on the math portion of the SAT without answering a single hard question.

Keep track of your current ability level so that you know the types of problems you should focus on. If you are currently scoring around a 400 on your practice tests, then you should be focusing primarily on Level 1, 2, and 3 problems. You can easily raise your score 100 points without having to practice a single hard problem.

If you are currently scoring about a 500, then your primary focus should be Level 2 and 3, but you should also do some Level 1 and 4 problems.

If you are scoring around a 600, you should be focusing on Level 2, 3, and 4 problems, but you should do some Level 1 and 5 problems as well.

Those of you at the 700 level really need to focus on those Level 4 and 5 problems.

If you really want to refine your studying, then you should keep track of your ability level in each of the four major categories of problems:

- **Heart of Algebra**
- **Passport to Advanced Math**
- **Problem Solving and Data Analysis**
- **Geometry and Complex Numbers**

For example, many students have trouble with easier Passport to Advanced Math problems, even though they can do difficult Heart of Algebra problems. This type of student may want to focus on Level 1, 2, and 3 Passport to Advanced Math questions, but Level 3 and 4 Heart of Algebra questions.

If you do not know your current score, you can take the 28-minute SAT Math Diagnostic Exam beginning on page 13. Then use the scoring guide on page 21 to calculate your approximate SAT math score. If you already know your current score, you can jump right into the problem sets.

Practice in small amounts over a long period of time: Ideally you want to practice doing SAT math problems for about ten to twenty minutes each day beginning at least 3 months before the exam. You will retain much more of what you study if you study in short bursts than if you try to tackle everything at once.

The only exception is on a day you do a practice test. You should do at least four practice tests before you take the SAT. Ideally you should do your practice tests on a Saturday or Sunday morning. At first you can do just the math sections. The last one or two times you take a practice test you should do the whole test in one sitting. As tedious as this is, it will prepare you for the amount of endurance that it will take to get through this exam.

2. Calculator use

- Use a TI-84 or comparable calculator if possible when practicing and during the SAT.
- Make sure that your calculator has fresh batteries on test day.
- You may have to switch between DEGREE and RADIAN modes during the test. If you are using a TI-84 (or equivalent) calculator press the MODE button and scroll down to the third line when necessary to switch between modes.

Below are the most important things you should practice on your graphing calculator.

- Practice entering complicated computations in a single step.
- Know when to insert parentheses:
  - Around numerators of fractions
  - Around denominators of fractions
  - Around exponents
  - Whenever you actually see parentheses in the expression

Examples:

We will substitute a 5 in for x in each of the following examples.

Expression	Calculator computation
$\dfrac{7x+3}{2x-11}$	$(7*5+3)/(2*5-11)$
$(3x-8)^{2x-9}$	$(3*5-8)\text{^}(2*5-9)$

- Clear the screen before using it in a new problem. The big screen allows you to check over your computations easily.
- Press the **ANS** button (**2ND (-)**) to use your last answer in the next computation.
- Press **2ND ENTER** to bring up your last computation for editing. This is especially useful when you are plugging in answer choices, or guessing and checking.
- You can press **2ND ENTER** over and over again to cycle backwards through all the computations you have ever done.
- Know where the $\sqrt{}$, π, and **^** buttons are so you can reach them quickly.
- Change a decimal to a fraction by pressing **MATH ENTER ENTER**.
- Press the **MATH** button - in the first menu, you can take cube roots and nth roots for any n.
- Know how to use the **SIN**, **COS**, and **TAN** buttons as well as **SIN^{-1}**, **COS^{-1}**, and **TAN^{-1}**.

You may find the following graphing tools useful.

- Press the **Y=** button to enter a function, and then hit **ZOOM 6** to graph it in a standard window.
- Practice using the **WINDOW** button to adjust the viewing window of your graph.
- Practice using the **TRACE** button to move along the graph and look at some of the points plotted.
- Pressing **2ND TRACE** (which is really **CALC**) will bring up a menu of useful items. For example, selecting **ZERO** will tell you where the graph hits the x-axis, or equivalently where the function is zero. Selecting **MINIMUM** or **MAXIMUM** can find the vertex of a parabola. Selecting **INTERSECT** will find the point of intersection of 2 graphs.

3. Tips for taking the SAT

Each of the following tips should be used whenever you take a practice SAT as well as on the actual exam.

Check your answers properly: When you go back to check your earlier answers for careless errors *do not* simply look over your work to try to catch a mistake. This is usually a waste of time.

- When "checking over" problems you have already done, **always redo the problem from the beginning** without looking at your earlier work.
- If possible, use a different method than you used the first time.

For example, if you solved the problem by picking numbers the first time, try to solve it algebraically the second time, or at the very least pick different numbers. If you do not know, or are not comfortable with a different method, then use the same method, but do the problem from the beginning and do not look at your original solution. If your two answers do not match up, then you know that this is a problem you need to spend a little more time on to figure out where your error is.

This may seem time consuming, but that is okay. It is better to spend more time checking over a few problems, than to rush through a lot of problems and repeat the same mistakes.

Take a guess whenever you cannot solve a problem: There is no guessing penalty on the SAT. Whenever you do not know how to solve a problem take a guess. Ideally you should eliminate as many answer choices as possible before taking your guess, but if you have no idea whatsoever, do not waste time overthinking. Simply put down an answer and move on. You should certainly mark it off and come back to it later if you have time.

Pace yourself: Do not waste your time on a question that is too hard or will take too long. After you've been working on a question for about 30 to 45 seconds you need to make a decision. If you understand the question and think that you can get the answer in another 30 seconds or so, continue to work on the problem. If you still do not know how to do the problem or you are using a technique that is going to take a long time, mark it off and come back to it later if you have time.

If you do not know the correct answer, eliminate as many answer choices as you can and take a guess. But you still want to leave open the possibility of coming back to it later. Remember that every problem is worth the same amount. Do not sacrifice problems that you may be able to do by getting hung up on a problem that is too hard for you.

Attempt the right number of questions: Many students make the mistake of thinking that they have to attempt every single SAT math question when they are taking the test. There is no such rule. In fact, many students will increase their SAT score by *reducing* the number of questions they attempt.

There are two math sections on the SAT—one where a calculator is allowed and one where a calculator is not allowed. The calculator section has 30 multiple choice (mc) questions and 8 free response (grid in) questions. The non-calculator section has 15 multiple choice (mc) questions and 5 free response (grid in) questions.

First, make sure that you know what you got on your last SAT practice test, actual SAT, or actual PSAT (whichever you took last). If you do not have any of those scores, you can take the 28-minute SAT Math Diagnostic Exam on page 13. What follows is a general goal you should go for when taking the exam.

Score	MC (Calculator Allowed)	Grid In (Calculator Allowed)	MC (Calculator Not Allowed)	Grid In (Calculator Not Allowed)
< 330	10/30	3/8	4/15	1/5
330 – 370	15/30	4/8	6/15	2/5
380 – 430	18/30	5/8	8/15	2/5
440 – 490	21/30	6/8	9/15	3/5
500 – 550	24/30	6/8	11/15	4/5
560 – 620	27/30	7/8	13/15	4/5
630 – 800	30/30	8/8	15/15	5/5

For example, a student with a current score of 570 should attempt 27 multiple choice questions and 7 grid ins from the section where a calculator is allowed, and 13 multiple choice questions and 4 grid in questions from the section where a calculator is not allowed.

This is *just* a general guideline. Of course, it can be fine-tuned. As a simple example, if you are particularly strong at Heart of Algebra problems, but very weak at Passport to Advanced Math problems, then you may want to try every Heart of Algebra problem no matter where it appears, and you may want to reduce the number of Passport to Advanced Math problems you attempt.

Remember that there is no guessing penalty on the SAT, so you should *not* leave any questions blank. This *does not* mean you should attempt every question. It means that if you are running out of time make sure you fill in answers for all the questions you did not have time to attempt.

Grid your answers correctly: The computer grades only what you have marked in the bubbles. The space above the bubbles is just for your convenience, and to help you do your bubbling correctly.

Never mark more than one circle in a column or the problem will automatically be marked wrong. You do not need to use all four columns. If you do not use a column just leave it blank.

The symbols that you can grid in are the digits 0 through 9, a decimal point, and a division symbol for fractions. Note that there is no negative symbol. So, answers to grid ins *cannot* be negative. Also, there are only four slots, so you cannot get an answer such as 52,326.

Sometimes there is more than one correct answer to a grid in question. Simply choose one of them to grid in. *Never* try to fit more than one answer into the grid.

If your answer is a whole number such as 2451 or a decimal that requires four or less slots such as 2.36, then simply enter the number starting at any column. The two examples just written must be started in the first column, but the number 16 can be entered starting in column 1, 2, or 3.

Note that there is no zero in column 1, so if your answer is 0 it must be gridded into column 2, 3, or 4.

Fractions can be gridded in any form as long as there are enough slots. The fraction $\frac{2}{100}$ must be reduced to $\frac{1}{50}$ simply because the first representation will not fit in the grid.

Fractions can also be converted to decimals before being gridded in. If a decimal cannot fit in the grid, then you can simply *truncate* it to fit. But you must use every slot in this case. For example, the decimal .167777777... can be gridded as .167, but .16 or .17 would both be marked wrong.

Instead of truncating decimals you can also *round* them. For example, the decimal above could be gridded as .168. Truncating is preferred because there is no thinking involved and you are less likely to make a careless error.

Here are three ways to grid in the number $\frac{8}{9}$.

Never grid in mixed numerals. If your answer is $2\frac{1}{4}$, and you grid in the mixed numeral $2\frac{1}{4}$, then this will be read as $\frac{21}{4}$ and will be marked wrong. You must either grid in the decimal 2.25 or the improper fraction $\frac{9}{4}$.

Here are two ways to grid in the mixed numeral $1\frac{1}{2}$ correctly.

SAT MATH DIAGNOSTIC EXAM

This diagnostic test was designed to give you a rough idea of what you would score in SAT math on the current version of the SAT. You can use this score as a starting point to decide the difficulty level of problems you should focus on. See page 8 for details.

Please take this diagnostic just as you would take the SAT. Notice that for the first part of the test a calculator is <u>not</u> allowed. For the second part of the test you may use a calculator. Please time yourself accurately and stop working as soon as your time is up. Continuing to answer questions after time is up will decrease the accuracy of your score. There is an answer key and scoring guide on page 21. Solutions to this diagnostic exam are included with your purchase of this book. See page 199 for details.

REFERENCE

For your convenience, here are the formulas that you will be given on the SAT. Feel free to look back at these formulas as you are taking the diagnostic exam.

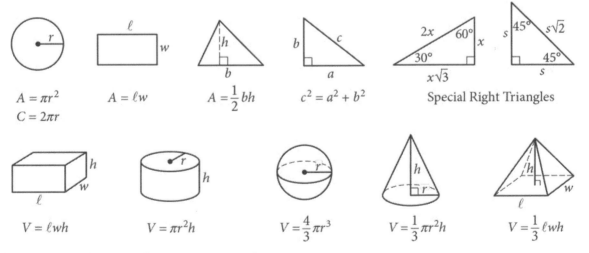

$A = \pi r^2$
$C = 2\pi r$

$A = \ell w$

$A = \frac{1}{2}bh$

$c^2 = a^2 + b^2$

Special Right Triangles

$V = \ell wh$

$V = \pi r^2 h$

$V = \frac{4}{3}\pi r^3$

$V = \frac{1}{3}\pi r^2 h$

$V = \frac{1}{3}\ell wh$

The number of degrees of arc in a circle is 360.
The number of radians of arc in a circle is 2π.
The sum of the measures in degrees of the angles of a triangle is 180.

Math Test – No Calculator

9 Minutes, 7 Questions

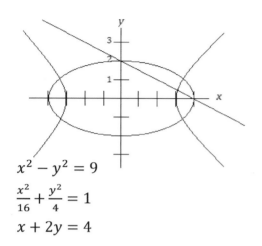

$$x^2 - y^2 = 9$$
$$\frac{x^2}{16} + \frac{y^2}{4} = 1$$
$$x + 2y = 4$$

1. A system of three equations in two unknowns and their graphs in the xy-plane are shown above. How many solutions does the system have?

    A) None
    B) Two
    C) Four
    D) Six

2. If $\frac{3}{x^2+2} = \frac{12}{z}$, where $z \neq 0$, what is z in terms of x ?

    A) $4x^2 + \frac{2}{3}$
    B) $4x^2 + 8$
    C) $4x^2 + 24$
    D) $\sqrt{\frac{3}{2}x - 2}$

    $3z = 12x^2 + 24$

    $z = 4x^2 + 8$

3. If -7 and 5 are both zeros of the polynomial $q(x)$, then a factor of $q(x)$ is

    A) $x^2 - 35$
    B) $x^2 + 35$
    C) $x^2 + 2x + 35$
    D) $x^2 + 2x - 35$

14

$$3x - 7y = 12$$
$$kx + 21y = -35$$

4. For which of the following values of k will the system of equations above have no solution?

   A) 9
   B) 3
   C) −3
   D) −9

6. If $\frac{1}{5}x + \frac{1}{7}y = 3$, what is the value of $7x + 5y$?

   105

$$g(x) = x^4 - kx^3 + 13x^2 - 12x + 4$$

7. The function g is defined above, and k is a constant. In the xy-plane, the graph of g intersects the y-axis at $(0,4)$ and intersects the x-axis at $(1,0)$ and $(2,0)$. What is the value of k?

   6

5. It is given that $\cos x = k$, where k is the radian measure of an angle and $\pi < x < \frac{3\pi}{2}$. If $\cos z = -k$, which of the following could <u>not</u> be the value of z ?

   A) $x - \pi$
   B) $\pi - x$
   C) $2\pi - x$
   D) $3\pi - x$

Math Test – Calculator

19 Minutes, 13 Questions

1. A high school has a $1000 budget to buy calculators. Each scientific calculator will cost the school $12.97 and each graphing calculator will cost the school $73.89. Which of the following inequalities represents the possible number of scientific calculators S and graphing calculators G that the school can purchase while staying within their specified budget?

   A) $12.97S + 73.89G > 1000$
   B) $12.97S + 73.89G \leq 1000$
   C) $\frac{12.97}{S} + \frac{73.89}{G} > 1000$
   D) $\frac{12.97}{S} + \frac{73.89}{G} \leq 1000$

2. A biologist was interested in the number of times a field cricket chirps each minute on a sunny day. He randomly selected 100 field crickets from a garden, and found that the mean number of chirps per minute was 112, and the margin of error for this estimate was 6 chirps. The biologist would like to repeat the procedure and attempt to reduce the margin of error. Which of the following samples would most likely result in a smaller margin of error for the estimated mean number of times a field cricket chirps each minute on a sunny day?

   A) 50 randomly selected crickets from the same garden.
   B) 50 randomly selected field crickets from the same garden.
   C) 200 randomly selected crickets from the same garden.
   D) 200 randomly selected field crickets from the same garden.

3. The expression $x^2 - x - 12$ can be written as the product of two binomial factors with integer coefficients. One of the binomials is $(x + 3)$. Which of the following is the other binomial?

   A) $x^2 - 4$
   B) $x^2 + 4$
   C) $x - 4$
   D) $x + 4$

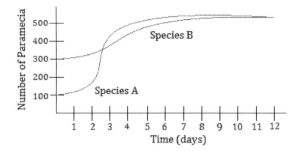

Paramecia present (in thousands) over twelve days

4. A small puddle is monitored by scientists for the number of *paramecia* present. The scientists are interested in two distinct species, let's call them "species *A*" and "species *B*." At time $t = 0$, the scientists measure and estimate the amount of species *A* and species *B* present in the puddle. They then proceed to measure and record the number of each species of *paramecium* present every hour for 12 days. The data for each species were then fit by a smooth curve, as shown in the graph above. Which of the following is a correct statement about the data above?

   A) At time $t = 0$, the number of species *B* present is 150% greater than the number of species *A* present.
   B) At time $t = 0$, the number of species *A* present is 75% less than the number of species *B* present.
   C) For the first 3 days, the average growth rate of species *B* is higher than the average growth rate of species *A*.
   D) The growth rate of both species *A* and species *B* decreases for the last 8 days.

5. If $y = k^{-\frac{2}{3}}$, where $k > y > 0$, which of the following equations gives k in terms of y ?

    A) $k = -\sqrt[3]{y^2}$

    B) $k = -\sqrt{y^3}$

    C) $k = \dfrac{1}{\sqrt[3]{y^2}}$

    D) $k = \dfrac{1}{\sqrt{y^3}}$

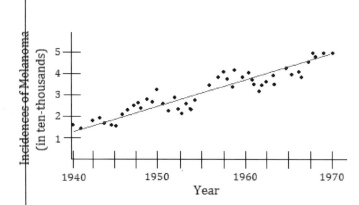

6. The scatterplot above shows the numbers of incidences of melanoma, in ten-thousands, from 1940 to 1970. Based on the line of best fit to the data, as shown in the figure, which of the following values is closest to the average yearly increase in the number of incidences of melanoma?

    A) 1300

    B) 330

    C) 0.33

    D) 0.13

$$2x + y = 7 - 2y$$
$$5y - x = 5 - 4x$$

7. If (x, y) is a solution to the above system of equations, what is the value of $\frac{y+1}{x}$?

    A) -11

    B) $-\dfrac{1}{2}$

    C) 2

    D) 20

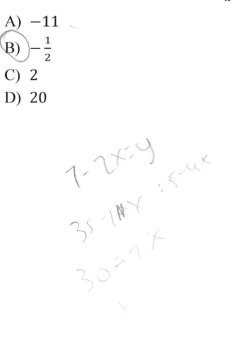

18

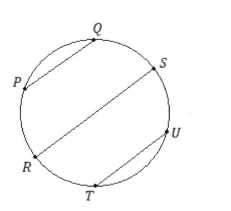

8. In the circle above with diameter d, chords $\overline{PQ}$ and $\overline{TU}$ are parallel to diameter $\overline{RS}$. If $\overline{PQ}$ and $\overline{TU}$ are each $\frac{3}{4}$ of the length of $\overline{RS}$, what is the distance between chords $\overline{PQ}$ and $\overline{TU}$ in terms of d ?

A) $\frac{d\sqrt{7}}{8}$

B) $\frac{d\sqrt{7}}{4}$

C) $\frac{\pi d}{4}$

D) $\frac{3\pi d}{4}$

9. 2500 single men and 2500 single women were asked about whether they owned any dogs or cats. The table below displays a summary of the results.

	Dogs Only	Cats Only	Both	Neither	Total
Men	920	270	50	1260	2500
Women	750	430	340	980	2500
Total	1670	700	390	2240	5000

Of the people who said they had neither dogs nor cats, 200 were selected at random, and they were asked if they had any pets at all. 43 people said they did have pets, and the remaining 157 said that they did not. Based on both the initial data given in the table, together with the new data stated in this paragraph, which of the following is most likely to be accurate?

A) Approximately 482 of the original people surveyed would say that they have no pets.

B) Approximately 1758 of the original people surveyed would say that they have no pets.

C) Approximately 1963 of the original people surveyed would say that they have no pets.

D) Approximately 3925 of the original people surveyed would say that they have no pets.

19

10. If the expression $\dfrac{9x^2}{3x+5}$ is written in the equivalent form $\dfrac{25}{3x+5} + k$, what is k in terms of x ?

    A) $9x^2$
    B) $9x^2 + 5$
    C) $3x - 5$
    D) $3x + 5$

$$\frac{7 - (4 - q)}{8} = \frac{3(5 - q)}{12}$$

11. In the equation above, what is the value of q ?

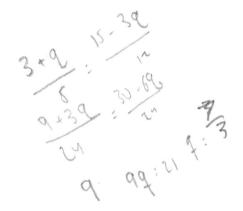

12. What is the sum of the two solutions of the equation $x^2 - 7x + 3 = 0$?

13. A biologist places a colony consisting of 5000 bacteria into a petri dish. After the initial placement of the bacteria at time $t = 0$, the biologist measures and estimates the number of bacteria present every half hour. This data was then fitted by an exponential curve of the form $y = c \cdot 2^{kt}$ where c and k are constants, t is measured in hours, and y is measured in thousands of bacteria. The scatterplot together with the exponential curve are shown below.

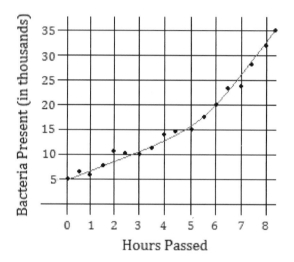

According to the scatterplot, the biologist's measurements indicate that the number of bacteria present quadrupled in 6 hours, and the exponential curve passes through the corresponding data point at time $t = 6$. The exponential function also agrees with the initial number of bacteria. Compute ck.

20

ANSWER KEY

Part 1

1. A
2. B
3. D
4. D
5. C
6. 105
7. 6

Part 2

1. B
2. D
3. C
4. D
5. D
6. A
7. B

8. B
9. B
10. C
11. 7/3 or 2.33
12. 7
13. 5/3, 1.66, or 1.67

SCORING

Add 1 point for each question you got correct. This sum is your **Raw Score**. Then use the conversion chart below to get your **Scaled Score**.

SAT Mathematics Conversion Table			
Raw Score	**Scaled Score**	**Raw Score**	**Scaled Score**
20	800		
19	750	9	490
18	700	8	470
17	670	7	440
16	650	6	420
15	620	5	400
14	600	4	370
13	580	3	340
12	560	2	300
11	530	1	260
10	520	0	200

PROBLEMS BY LEVEL AND TOPIC WITH SOLUTIONS
PROBLEM SET A

LEVEL 1: HEART OF ALGEBRA

1. If $5 - 11x = 11x + 5$, what is the value of x ?

    A) 0
    B) 1
    C) 2.2
    D) 3

(Solving Linear Equations)

Solution by plugging in answer choices: Normally we would start with choice B or C as our first guess, but in this case, it's not too hard to see that 0 satisfies the equation. Indeed, we see that we have $5 - 11 \cdot 0 = 5$ and $11 \cdot 0 + 5 = 5$. So, $x = 0$, choice **A**.

Notes: (1) A basic SAT math strategy that every student should know is "plugging in the answer choices." To use this strategy, we simply try out each answer choice until we find the one that "works." If we have no other information we would generally start with choice B or C as our first guess. In this particular problem, a little thought should quickly lead you to choice A.

(2) If we try choice C first, then the left-hand side of the equation gives us $5 - 11 \cdot 1 = 5 - 11 = -6$ and the right-hand side of the equation gives us $11 \cdot 1 + 5 = 11 + 5 = 16$. Since $-6 \neq 16$, we can eliminate choice C.

* Algebraic solution: We can strike off a 5 from each side of the equation to get $-11x = 11x$. We then add $11x$ to each side of this last equation to get $0 = 11x + 11x = 22x$. Dividing each side by 22, we have $x = \frac{0}{22} = 0$, choice **A**.

Notes: (1) If the same quantity appears on each side of an equation, we can simply *strike it off from each side*. In this problem, 5 appears on each side of the equation, and so, we can simply delete it from each side.

(2) You can physically use your pencil to strike off those 5's. The marked-up problem would look as follows.

$$\cancel{5} - 11x = 11x + \cancel{5}$$

(3) Once you strike off the 5's, it may become clear to you that 0 is the answer. If not, it's okay. Just proceed to add $11x$ to each side of the equation to get $0 = 22x$.

(4) Informal reasoning can be used in the last step to save a bit of time. The equation $22x = 0$ can be read as "22 times what is 0?" Well, 22 times 0 is 0, and so the answer is 0.

2. A bank charges a fee of $10 per month to have an account. In addition, there is a charge of $0.05 per check written. Which of the following represents the total charge, in dollars, to have an account for one month in which n checks have been written?

  A) $0.95n$
  B) $1.05n$
  C) $10.00 + 5n$
  D) $10.00 + 0.05n$

(Setting Up Linear Expressions)

Solution by picking a number: Let's choose a value for n, say $n = 4$. The total charge for the account including the checks written is then $\$10 + \$0.20 = \$10.20$ **Put a nice, big, dark circle around the number 10.20.** Now substitute 4 in for n in each answer choice and eliminate any answer that does not come out to 10.20.

  A) $0.95(4) = 3.8$
  B) $1.05(4) = 4.2$
  C) $10.00 + 5(4) = 30$
  D) $10.00 + 0.05(4) = 10.20$

Since choices A, B, and C came out incorrect, the answer is choice **D**.

Notes: (1) D is **not** the correct answer simply because it is equal to 10.20. It is correct because all three of the other choices are **not** 10.20. **You must check all four choices!**

(2) All the above computations can be done in a single step with your calculator (if a calculator is allowed for this problem).

(3) We picked a number that was simple, but not too simple. In general, we might want to avoid 0 and 1 because more than one choice is likely to come out correct with these choices. Numbers between 2 and 10 are usually good choices.

(4) When using the strategy of picking numbers, it is very important that we check every answer choice. It is possible for more than one choice to come out to the correct answer. We would then need to pick new numbers to try to eliminate all but one choice.

* Algebraic solution: The total charge is $10.00 for the account, plus $0.05n$ for the checks. This is $10.00 + 0.05n$ dollars, choice **D**.

Notes: (1) If 1 check is written, then the cost for the check is 0.05 dollars.

If 2 checks are written, the cost for the checks is $0.05 \cdot 2 = 0.10$ dollars.

If 3 checks are written, the cost for the checks is $0.05 \cdot 3 = 0.15$ dollars.

Following this pattern, we see that if n checks are written, the cost for the checks is $0.05n$ dollars.

(2) Don't forget to add in the charge of 10 dollars at the end to get a total of $10 + 0.05n$ dollars.

3. In the xy-plane, what is the slope of the line that passes through the points $(0, 0)$ and $(-5, -3)$?

    A) -5

    B) -3

    C) $\frac{3}{5}$

    D) $\frac{5}{3}$

(Equations of Lines and Their Graphs)

Solution by drawing a picture: We plot the two points as shown to the right and observe that to get from $(-5, -3)$ to $(0, 0)$ we move up 3 and right 5. So, the answer is $\frac{3}{5}$, choice **C**.

Solution using the slope formula: $\frac{-3-0}{-5-0} = \frac{-3}{-5} = \frac{3}{5}$, choice **C**.

Notes: (1) The slope of the line passing through the points (x_1, y_1) and (x_2, y_2) is

$$\text{Slope} = m = \frac{\text{rise}}{\text{run}} = \frac{y_2 - y_1}{x_2 - x_1}$$

Here, the points are $(x_1, y_1) = (-5, -3)$ and $(x_2, y_2) = (0, 0)$.

(2) Lines with **positive slope** have graphs that go upwards from left to right.

Lines with **negative slope** have graphs that go downwards from left to right.

Horizontal lines have **zero slope**.

Vertical lines have **no slope** (or **infinite slope** or **undefined slope**).

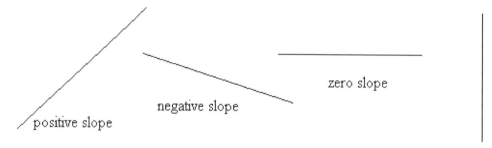

positive slope   negative slope   zero slope   no slope

* Quicker slope computation: The slope is $\frac{-3}{-5} = \frac{3}{5}$, choice **C**.

Note: If the line j passes through the origin (the point $(0, 0)$) and the point (c, d) with $c \neq 0$, then the slope of line j is simply $\frac{d}{c}$. In other words, if a line passes through the origin, then we can get the slope very quickly by taking any other point on the line and dividing its y-coordinate by its x-coordinate.

4. Which of the following equations represents a line that is perpendicular to the line with equation $y = -3x - 21$?

A) $y = -3x + \frac{1}{21}$

B) $y = 3x + 15$

C) $y = -\frac{1}{3}x + 7$

D) $y = \frac{1}{3}x + 1$

(Equations of Lines and Their Graphs)

* The slope of the line whose equation is given is -3. Therefore, the slope of a line perpendicular to the given one is $\frac{1}{3}$. It follows that the answer is choice **D**.

Notes: (1) Recall that the slope-intercept form of an equation of a line is $y = mx + b$, where m is the slope of the line.

For example, the equation $y = -3x - 21$ is an equation of a line in slope-intercept form, and the line has slope $m = -3$.

(2) Perpendicular lines have slopes that are negative reciprocals of each other.

(3) The reciprocal of -3 is $-\frac{1}{3}$, and the negative reciprocal of -3 is $-\left(-\frac{1}{3}\right) = \frac{1}{3}$.

(4) The slope-intercept form of the equation of a line with slope $\frac{1}{3}$ is $y = \frac{1}{3}x + b$ for some real number b. Only choice D has this form.

5. Which of the following is equivalent to $5(x - 3) - (x - 1) + 4$?

A) $4x + 8$

B) $4x$

C) $4x - 10$

D) $16x + 4$

(Manipulating Linear Expressions)

* **Algebraic solution:**

$$5(x - 3) - (x - 1) + 4 = 5x - 15 - x + 1 + 4 = (5x - x) + (-15 + 1 + 4) = 4x - 10.$$

This is choice **C**.

Notes: (1) The **distributive property** says that for all real numbers a, b, and c,

$$a(b + c) = ab + ac$$

More specifically, this property says that the operation of multiplication distributes over addition. The distributive property is very important, as it allows us to multiply and factor algebraic expressions.

We used the distributive property twice in this problem:

$$5(x - 3) = 5x - 15 \qquad -(x - 1) = -x + 1$$

(2) Many students fail to apply the distributive property correctly. For example, it is common for students to write $5(x - 3) = 5x - 3$ and $-(x - 1) = -x - 1$. Make sure that you are aware that these two equations are **not** correct.

(3) This problem can also be solved by picking numbers. This would be a bit time consuming here, but you still might want to practice it. I leave this solution as an exercise for the reader.

$$x + 5 + x + 2x = x + x + x + 3 + 5x$$

6. In the equation above, what is the value of x ?

(Solving Linear Equations)

* Algebraic solution: Let's start by striking off two x's from each side of the equation to get

$$5 + 2x = x + 3 + 5x$$

We now combine like terms on the right to get $5 + 2x = 3 + 6x$. We then subtract $2x$ from each side of the equation and subtract 3 from each side of the equation to get $2 = 4x$. Finally, we divide each side of this last equation by 2 to get $x = \frac{2}{4} = \mathbf{1/2}$ or $\mathbf{.5}$.

Notes: (1) See Problem 1 above to learn the technique of "striking off."

(2) Informal reasoning can be used in the last step to save a bit of time. The equation $4x = 2$ can be read as "4 times what is 2?" Well, 4 times $\frac{1}{2}$ is 2, and so, the answer is $1/2$.

7. Each cat in an adoption center is given 2 toys and there are 11 additional toys stored in a closet. There are no other toys in the center. If there are at least 23 but no more than 29 toys in the adoption center, what is one possible value for the number of cats in the adoption center?

(Solving Linear Inequalities)

Solution by guessing: Let's take a guess that there are 5 cats in the adoption center. Then there is a total of $5 \cdot 2 + 11 = 10 + 11 = 21$ toys. This is too few.

Let's next guess that there are 7 cats in the adoption center. It then follows that there is a total of $7 \cdot 2 + 11 = 14 + 11 = 25$ toys. Since 25 is between 23 and 29, we can grid in **7**.

* Algebraic solution: If we let c be the number of cats in the adoption center, then we have $23 \leq 2c + 11 \leq 29$. We solve for c.

$$23 \leq 2c + 11 \leq 29$$
$$12 \leq 2c \leq 18$$
$$6 \leq c \leq 9$$

So, we can grid in **6, 7, 8** or **9**.

$$5y = x$$
$$5y = 70 - x$$

8. Based on the system of equations above, what is the value of x ?

(Solving Linear Systems of Equations)

* Algebraic solution: Since x and $70 - x$ are both equal to the same quantity, they are equal to each other. So, we have $x = 70 - x$. Adding x to each side of this equation gives us $2x = 70$. Finally, we divide each side of this last equation by 2 to get $x = \mathbf{35}$.

LEVEL 1: PASSPORT TO ADVANCED MATH

9. If the expression $3ab + 12$ is equivalent to $3(ab + c)$, where a, b, and c are constants, what is the value of c ?

    A) 1
    B) 2
    C) 4
    D) 6

(Factoring)

* Solution by factoring: $3ab + 12 = 3(ab + 4)$

So, $c = 4$, and the answer is choice **C**.

Notes: (1) Factoring is just the distributive property in reverse. Recall from Problem 5 above that the **distributive property** says that $x(y + z) = xy + xz$. In this problem, we have $x = 3$, $y = ab$, and $z = c$. We have $xz = 3c$ and we also have $xz = 12$. So, $3c = 12$, and therefore, $c = \frac{12}{3} = 4$.

(2) This problem can also be solved by picking numbers. I leave the details to the reader.

10. Which of the following is equivalent to $(x^2)^4 x^3$?

    A) x^5
    B) x^6
    C) x^9
    D) x^{11}

(Exponents and Roots)

* Solution using laws of exponents:
$$(x^2)^4 x^3 = x^8 x^3 = x^{11}.$$

The answer is choice **D**.

Notes: (1) For the first step, we used the law of exponents in the fifth row of the table below (see Note 4) to write $(x^2)^4 = x^{2\cdot4} = x^8$.

(2) $(x^2)^4$ means multiply x^2 by itself 4 times: $(x^2)^4 = x^2 x^2 x^2 x^2 = (x \cdot x)(x \cdot x)(x \cdot x)(x \cdot x) = x^8$. This kind of reasoning can be used if you ever forget an exponential law.

(3) For the second step, we used the law of exponents in the third row of the table below (again, see Note 4) to write $x^8 x^3 = x^{8+3} = x^{11}$.

(4) Here is a brief review of the laws of exponents you should know for the SAT.

Law	Example
$x^0 = 1$	$3^0 = 1$
$x^1 = x$	$9^1 = 9$
$x^a x^b = x^{a+b}$	$x^3 x^5 = x^8$
$x^a / x^b = x^{a-b}$	$x^{11}/x^4 = x^7$
$(x^a)^b = x^{ab}$	$(x^5)^3 = x^{15}$
$(xy)^a = x^a y^a$	$(xy)^4 = x^4 y^4$
$(x/y)^a = x^a / y^a$	$(x/y)^6 = x^6 / y^6$
$x^{-1} = 1/x$	$3^{-1} = 1/3$
$x^{-a} = 1/x^a$	$9^{-2} = 1/81$
$x^{1/n} = \sqrt[n]{x}$	$x^{1/3} = \sqrt[3]{x}$
$x^{m/n} = \sqrt[n]{x^m} = \left(\sqrt[n]{x}\right)^m$	$x^{9/2} = \sqrt{x^9} = \left(\sqrt{x}\right)^9$

11. If $\dfrac{5x^2}{2y} = \dfrac{15}{4}$, what is the value of $\dfrac{x^2}{y}$?

A) $\dfrac{2}{3}$

B) $\dfrac{3}{4}$

C) $\dfrac{3}{2}$

D) $\dfrac{75}{8}$

(Manipulating Nonlinear Expressions)

Algebraic solution: We multiply each side of the given equation by $\frac{2}{5}$ to get $\frac{x^2}{y} = \frac{15}{4} \cdot \frac{2}{5} = \frac{2}{4} \cdot \frac{15}{5} = \frac{3}{2}$, choice **C**.

Notes: (1) We define a **block** to be an algebraic expression that appears more than once in a given problem. Very often in SAT problems a block can be treated just like a variable. In particular, blocks should usually not be manipulated—treat them as a single unit.

In this question, there is a block of $\frac{x^2}{y}$ because it appears twice. The question is really just asking $\frac{5}{2}$ times what is $\frac{15}{4}$? In this solution, we informally found the "what" by looking at the numerator and denominator separately.

(2) There is no need to find x here, as x^2 is part of the block. Solving for x would be "breaking the block," which we should always avoid.

* Solution by picking numbers with informal algebra: Since $5 \cdot 3 = 15$, it seems like a good choice would be $x^2 = 3$, and since $2 \cdot 2 = 4$, another good choice would be $y = 2$. We then have $\frac{x^2}{y} = \frac{3}{2}$, choice **C**.

12. If $k^2 - 31 = 17 - 2k^2$, what are all possible values of k ?

A) 4 only
B) −4 only
C) 0 only
D) 4 and −4 only

(Solving Quadratic Equations)

Solution by plugging in the answer choices: According to the answer choices we need only check 0, 4, and −4.

$k = 0$: $\quad 0^2 - 31 = 17 - 2(0)^2$ $\quad -31 = 17$ $\quad$ False

$k = 4$: $\quad 4^2 - 31 = 17 - 2(4)^2$ $\quad -15 = -15$ $\quad$ True

$k = -4$: $\quad (-4)^2 - 31 = 17 - 2(-4)^2$ $\quad -15 = -15$ $\quad$ True

So, the answer is choice **D**.

Notes: (1) Since all powers of k in the given equation are even, 4 and −4 must give the same answer. So, we didn't really need to check −4.

(2) The following table reviews the correct **order of operations**.

PEMDAS	
P	Parentheses
E	Exponentiation
M	Multiplication
D	Division
A	Addition
S	Subtraction

Note that multiplication and division have the same priority, and addition and subtraction have the same priority.

(3) Observe that when performing the computations above, the proper order of operations was followed (see Note 2 above). Exponentiation was done first, followed by multiplication, and then subtraction was done last.

For example, we have $4^2 - 31 = 16 - 31 = -15$ and $17 - 2(4)^2 = 17 - 2 \cdot 16 = 17 - 32 = -15$.

* Algebraic solution: We add $2k^2$ to each side of the given equation to get $3k^2 - 31 = 17$. We then add 31 to get $3k^2 = 17 + 31 = 48$. Dividing each side of this last equation by 3 gives $k^2 = \frac{48}{3} = 16$. We now use the **square root property** to get $k = \pm 4$. So, the answer is choice **D**.

Notes: (1) The equation $k^2 = 16$ has two solutions: $k = 4$ and $k = -4$. A common mistake is to forget about the negative solution.

(2) The **square root property** says that if $x^2 = c$, then $x = \pm\sqrt{c}$.

This is different from taking the positive square root of a number. For example, $\sqrt{16} = 4$, while the equation $x^2 = 16$ has two solutions $x = \pm 4$.

(3) Another way to solve the equation $k^2 = 16$ is to subtract 16 from each side of the equation, and then factor the difference of two squares as follows:

$$k^2 - 16 = 0$$
$$(k - 4)(k + 4) = 0$$

We now set each factor equal to 0 to get $k - 4 = 0$ or $k + 4 = 0$. Thus, $k = 4$ or $k = -4$.

$$y = 2x$$
$$x = y^2$$

13. Which of the following ordered pairs is a solution to the system of equations above?

A) $(-\frac{1}{4}, \frac{1}{2})$

B) $(-\frac{1}{4}, -\frac{1}{2})$

C) $(\frac{1}{4}, -\frac{1}{2})$

D) $(\frac{1}{4}, \frac{1}{2})$

(Nonlinear Systems of Equations)

* Solution by plugging in answer choices: Normally we would start with choice B or C, but in this case, since there are no minus signs in the given equations, it seems like choice D would be the best guess. So, let's guess that $x = \frac{1}{4}$ and $y = \frac{1}{2}$. Then the first equation gives us $\frac{1}{2} = 2 \cdot \frac{1}{4}$, and the second equation gives us $\frac{1}{4} = \left(\frac{1}{2}\right)^2$. Since both equations are true, the answer is choice **D**.

Complete algebraic solution: Using the first equation, $y = 2x$, we can replace y by $2x$ in the second equation to get $x = (2x)^2 = 4x^2$. We subtract x from each side of this equation to get $4x^2 - x = 0$. We factor the left-hand side of this equation to get $x(4x - 1) = 0$. So, $x = 0$ or $4x - 1 = 0$. Adding 1 to each side of this last equation gives us $4x = 1$, and then dividing each side by 4 yields $x = \frac{1}{4}$. Using the first equation once more, we have $y = 2x = 2 \cdot \frac{1}{4} = \frac{1}{2}$. So $(\frac{1}{4}, \frac{1}{2})$ is a solution to the given system, choice **D**.

Note: We can also use the second equation, $x = y^2$, and replace x by y^2 in the first equation. This would give us $y = 2y^2$, so that $2y^2 - y = 0$. We can then factor the left-hand side of this expression to get $y(2y - 1) = 0$, so that $y = 0$ or $y = \frac{1}{2}$. Using $y = \frac{1}{2}$, we get $x = y^2 = \left(\frac{1}{2}\right)^2 = \frac{1}{4}$. This also shows that $\left(\frac{1}{4}, \frac{1}{2}\right)$ is a solution to the given system, giving us choice D as the answer.

14. For the function $f(x) = 2x^2 - 3x - 1$, what is the value of $f(-2)$?

(Functions)

* $f(-2) = 2(-2)^2 - 3(-2) - 1 = 2 \cdot 4 + 6 - 1 = 8 + 6 - 1 = 14 - 1 = \mathbf{13}$.

Notes: (1) To square a number means to multiply it by itself. So, $(-2)^2 = (-2)(-2) = 4$. Many students get this confused with the computation $-2^2 = (-1)(2)(2) = -4$.

(2) The exponentiation was done first, followed by the multiplication. Addition was done last. See the notes after Problem 12 for more information on order of operations.

(3) If a calculator is allowed, we can do the whole computation in our calculator in one step. Simply type $2(-2)^2 - 3(-2) - 1$ ENTER. The output will be 13.

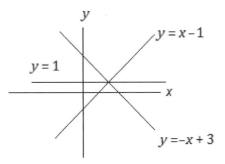

15. Three equations and their graphs in the xy-plane are shown above. How many solutions does the system consisting of those three equations have?

(Graphs of Functions)

* From the graphs, we see that this system has one solution. It is the point of intersection of all 3 graphs. The answer is **1**.

Notes: (1) The figure shows three graphs in the xy-plane. These are the graphs of the following system of equations:

$$\begin{aligned} y &= x - 1 \\ y &= -x + 3 \\ y &= 1 \end{aligned}$$

(2) To find the point of intersection of the three graphs, first observe that all three points must have y-coordinate 1 (because $y = 1$ is one of the equations). We can now substitute $y = 1$ into either of the other two equations to find x. For example, $1 = x - 1$ implies that $x = 2$. So, the only solution to the given system is $(\mathbf{2}, \mathbf{1})$.

(3) Let's just check that the point $(2, 1)$ is also on the graph of the equation $y = -x + 3$. If we substitute 2 for x, we get $y = -2 + 3 = 1$.

16. The sum of $5x^2 - 1$ and $-2x + 1$ can be written as $ax^2 + bx + c$. What is the value of abc ?

(Operations on Polynomials)

* Algebraic solution: $(5x^2 - 1) + (-2x + 1) = 5x^2 - 1 - 2x + 1 = 5x^2 - 2x + 0$. So, $a = 5$, $b = -2$, and $c = 0$. Therefore, $abc = 5(-2) \cdot 0 = \mathbf{0}$.

LEVEL 1: PROBLEM SOLVING

17. Joe has decided to walk dogs to earn some extra money. He makes the same amount of money for each dog he walks. If he earns \$360 in a week for which he walks 30 dogs, how much does he earn, in dollars, for each dog he walks?

   A) \$2
   B) \$4
   C) \$6
   D) \$12

(Ratios)

Solution by setting up a ratio: (Step 1) We identify 2 key words. Let's choose "dollars" and "dogs."

(Step 2) Next to the word "dollars" we put the number 360 for the amount Joe earns for walking 30 dogs, followed by x for the unknown number of dollars he earns for walking 1 dog. Then, next to the word dogs, we put 30, followed by 1. Here is how it should look:

dollars	360	x
dogs	30	1

Note that it is important that the 30 goes under the 360 and the 1 goes under the x.

(Step 3) We now draw in 2 division symbols and an equal sign.

$$\frac{360}{30} = \frac{x}{1}$$

(Step 4) Finally, we find x by cross multiplying and then dividing.

$$30x = 360$$
$$x = \frac{360}{30} = 12$$

This is choice **D**.

* Quick solution: $\frac{360}{30} = 12$, choice **D**.

Questions 18 - 20 refer to the following information.

A survey was conducted among a randomly chosen sample of 100 males and 100 females to gather data on family size. The data are shown in the table below.

	Have siblings	Do not have siblings	Total
Men	75	25	100
Women	63	37	100
Total	138	62	200

18. How many of the women surveyed do not have siblings?

    A) 25
    B) 37
    C) 62
    D) 63

(Tables)

* We look at the row labeled "Women" and the column labeled "Do not have siblings." The answer is 37, choice **B**.

Note: The appropriate entry is highlighted in the table below.

	Have siblings	Do not have siblings	Total
Men	75	25	100
Women	63	37	100
Total	138	62	200

19. Which of the following is closest to the percent of those surveyed who have siblings?

    A) 31
    B) 63
    C) 69
    D) 75

(Tables and Percents)

* 200 people were surveyed, and 138 have siblings. So, the answer is $\frac{138}{200} \cdot 100 = 69\%$, choice **C**.

Notes: (1) To compute a percentage, use the simple formula

$$\text{Percentage} = \frac{\text{Part}}{\text{Whole}} \times 100$$

In this problem the *Part* is 138 and the *Whole* is 200.

(2) Alternatively, we can simply divide the *Part* by the *Whole* in our calculator and then change the resulting decimal to a percent by moving the decimal point to the right two places.

$$\frac{\text{Part}}{\text{Whole}} = \frac{138}{200} = 0.69 = 69\%$$

20. A man who was surveyed is randomly selected. What is the probability that he has siblings?

   A) $\frac{1}{4}$

   B) $\frac{1}{2}$

   C) $\frac{3}{4}$

   D) 1

(Tables and Probability)

* Solution using the simple probability principle: There were a total of 100 men surveyed. 75 of these men have siblings. So, the desired probability is $\frac{75}{100} = \frac{3}{4}$, choice **C**.

Note: To compute a simple probability where all outcomes are equally likely, we divide the number of "successes" by the total number of outcomes. This is called the **simple probability principle**.

In this problem, a "success" would be selecting a man who has siblings. The number of successes can be found by looking in the row labeled "Men" and the column labeled "Have Siblings." So, the number of successes is 75.

The "total" is the number of men surveyed. This number can be found in the row labeled "Men" and the column labeled "Total." So, the total is 100.

21. For which of the following lists of 5 numbers is the average (arithmetic mean) greater than the median?

   A) $4, 4, 5, 6, 6$
   B) $3, 4, 5, 7, 8$
   C) $3, 3, 5, 7, 7$
   D) $3, 4, 5, 6, 7$

(Statistics)

* All four answer choices have a median of 5. Choices A, C, and D all have numbers that are equally balanced to the left and the right of the median. So, for these choices the average is equal to the median. Therefore, the answer is choice **B**.

Notes: (1) If you don't follow the reasoning in the above solution, you can simply compute the averages in each answer choice until you find one that is bigger than 5. For example, the average of the number in choice B is $\frac{3+4+5+7+8}{5} = \frac{27}{5} = 5.4$.

(2) Alternatively, we can use the strategy of **changing averages to sums**. Since we want the average to be greater than 5, we want the sum to be greater than $5 \cdot 5 = 25$. If we add up the numbers in choice B, we get $3 + 4 + 5 + 7 + 8 = 27$, which is greater than 25.

Definitions: The **average (arithmetic mean)** of a list of numbers is the sum of the numbers in the list divided by the quantity of the numbers in the list.

$$\textbf{Average} = \frac{\textbf{Sum}}{\textbf{Number}}$$

On the SAT, it is often useful to rewrite this formula as

$$\textbf{Sum} = \textbf{Average} \cdot \textbf{Number}$$

The **median** of a list of numbers is the middle number when the numbers are arranged in increasing order. If the total number of values in the list is even, then the median is the average of the two middle values.

22. If y years and 11 months is equal to 551 months, what is the value of y ?

(Ratios)

* Quick solution: $y = \frac{(551-11)}{12} = \frac{540}{12} = \textbf{45}$.

Notes: (1) There are 12 months in a year. So, 45 years is $45 \cdot 12 = 540$ months.

When we add 11 months to 540 months, we get $540 + 11 = 551$ months.

(2) Saying that "y years and 11 months is equal to 551 months" is equivalent to saying that "y years is equal to 540 months." We get from 551 to 540 by subtracting 11.

(3) We convert 540 months to years by dividing 540 by 12.

(4) We can also convert from months to years by formally setting up a ratio as follows.

months	540	12
years	x	1

$$\frac{540}{x} = \frac{12}{1} \Rightarrow 12x = 540 \Rightarrow x = \frac{540}{12} = 45$$

Questions 23 - 24 refer to the following information.

A hose is being used to empty a pool. The graph below gives the number of gallons of water in the pool from the beginning to the end of this process.

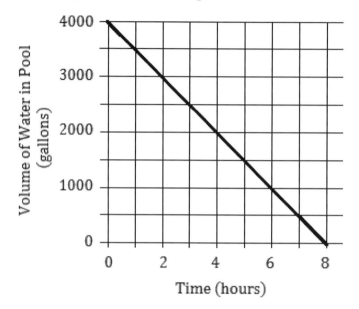

23. According to the graph, how many gallons of water were initially in the pool?

(Graphs)

* The initial amount of water in the pool occurs at time 0. At this time, the number of gallons is **4000**.

24. According to the graph, how long did it take, in hours, to empty the entire pool?

(Graphs)

* The pool is empty when the volume of the water in the pool is 0. This occurs after 8 hours. So, we grid in **8**.

LEVEL 1: GEOMETRY AND COMPLEX NUMBERS

25. Given that C is the midpoint of line segment $\overline{AB}$, $AB = 3$, $AC = x$, and $CB = 2y$, what is the value of y ?

    A) 0.5
    B) 0.75
    C) 1.5
    D) 1.75

(Lines and Angles)

* Let's draw a figure.

A — x — C — $2y$ — B

3

Since $AB = 3$, $2y = \frac{1}{2}AB = \frac{1}{2} \cdot 3 = 1.5$. So, $y = \frac{1.5}{2} = 0.75$, choice **B**.

Note: The **midpoint** of a line segment lies midway between the two points of the segment, and thus, it splits the segment in half.

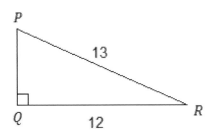

26. Given right triangle ΔPQR above, what is the length of $\overline{PQ}$?

    A) $\sqrt{2}$
    B) $\sqrt{5}$
    C) 5
    D) 7

(Triangles)

Solution by the Pythagorean Theorem: By the Pythagorean Theorem, we have $13^2 = (PQ)^2 + 12^2$. So, $169 = (PQ)^2 + 144$. Subtracting 144 from each side of this equation yields $25 = (PQ)^2$, or $PQ = 5$, choice **C**.

Remarks: (1) The Pythagorean Theorem says that if a right triangle has legs of lengths a and b, and a hypotenuse of length c, then $c^2 = a^2 + b^2$.

(2) Be careful in this problem: the length of the hypotenuse is 13. The hypotenuse is always opposite the right angle. So, we replace c by 13 in the Pythagorean Theorem.

(3) The equation $x^2 = 25$ would normally have two solutions: $x = 5$ and $x = -5$. But the length of a side of a triangle cannot be negative, so we reject -5.

* Solution using Pythagorean triples: We use the Pythagorean triple $5, 12, 13$ to see that $PQ = 5$, choice **C**.

Note: A **Pythagorean triple** is a set of three numbers that satisfy the Pythagorean Theorem. The most common Pythagorean triples are $3, 4, 5$ and $5, 12, 13$. Two others are $8, 15, 17$ and $7, 24, 25$.

27. A container in the shape of a right circular cylinder has a height of 3 inches and a base radius of 4 inches. What is the volume, in cubic inches, of the container?

    A) 12π
    B) 18π
    C) 36π
    D) 48π

(Solid Geometry)

* Since the container is shaped like a cylinder, its volume is

$$V = \pi r^2 h = \pi(4)^2 \cdot 3 = \pi \cdot 16 \cdot 3 = 48\pi.$$

This is choice **D**.

Note: The volume of a cylinder with base radius r and height h is $\boldsymbol{V = \pi r^2 h}$.

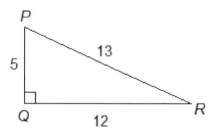

28. In the figure above, which of the following trigonometric expressions has value $\frac{12}{5}$?

    A) $\sin R$
    B) $\cos R$
    C) $\tan R$
    D) $\tan P$

(Trigonometry)

Solution by plugging in answer choices: Let's start with choice C and compute $\tan R = \frac{\text{OPP}}{\text{ADJ}} = \frac{5}{12}$. This is incorrect, and so we can eliminate choice C.

However, observe that we got the reciprocal of what we are looking for. So, it is natural to try choice D next. In this case, we have $\tan P = \frac{\text{OPP}}{\text{ADJ}} = \frac{12}{5}$. This is correct, and so the answer is choice **D**.

Note: In the above solution, OPP stands for "opposite" and ADJ stands for "adjacent."

* **Quick solution:** Note that the numerator and denominator of the fraction are the lengths of the leg opposite to P and adjacent to P, respectively. So, the answer is $\frac{\text{OPP}}{\text{ADJ}} = \tan P$, choice **D**.

Here is a quick lesson in **right triangle trigonometry** for those of you that have forgotten.

Let's begin by focusing on angle A in the following picture:

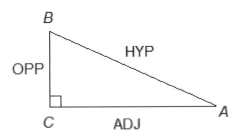

Note that the **hypotenuse** is ALWAYS the side opposite the right angle.

The other two sides of the right triangle, called the **legs**, depend on which angle is chosen. In this picture we chose to focus on angle A. Therefore, the opposite side is BC, and the adjacent side is AC.

Now you should simply memorize how to compute the six trig functions:

$$\sin A = \frac{\text{OPP}}{\text{HYP}} \qquad \csc A = \frac{\text{HYP}}{\text{OPP}}$$

$$\cos A = \frac{\text{ADJ}}{\text{HYP}} \qquad \sec A = \frac{\text{HYP}}{\text{ADJ}}$$

$$\tan A = \frac{\text{OPP}}{\text{ADJ}} \qquad \cot A = \frac{\text{ADJ}}{\text{OPP}}$$

Here are a couple of tips to help you remember these:

(1) Many students find it helpful to use the word SOHCAHTOA. You can think of the letters here as representing sin, opp, hyp, cos, adj, hyp, tan, opp, adj.

(2) The three trig functions on the right are the reciprocals of the three trig functions on the left. In other words, you get them by interchanging the numerator and denominator. It's easy to remember that the reciprocal of tangent is cotangent. For the other two, just remember that the "s" goes with the "c" and the "c" goes with the "s." In other words, the reciprocal of sine is cosecant, and the reciprocal of cosine is secant.

To make sure you understand this, compute all six trig functions for each of the angles (except the right angle) in the triangle given in this problem. Please try this yourself before looking at the answers below.

$$\sin P = \frac{12}{13} \qquad \csc P = \frac{13}{12} \qquad \sin R = \frac{5}{13} \qquad \csc R = \frac{13}{5}$$

$$\cos P = \frac{5}{13} \qquad \sec P = \frac{13}{5} \qquad \cos R = \frac{12}{13} \qquad \sec R = \frac{13}{12}$$

$$\tan P = \frac{12}{5} \qquad \cot P = \frac{5}{12} \qquad \tan R = \frac{5}{12} \qquad \cot R = \frac{12}{5}$$

29. The product of the complex numbers i and $1 - 3i$ is written in the form $a + bi$, where a and b are real numbers and $i = \sqrt{-1}$. What is the value of b ?

    A) -3
    B) -1
    C) 1
    D) 3

(Complex Numbers)

* $i(1 - 3i) = i - 3i^2 = i - 3(-1) = i + 3 = 3 + i$. So, $b = 1$, choice **C**.

Notes: (1) The numbers $i = 0 + 1i$ and $1 - 3i$ are **complex numbers**. In general, a complex number has the form $a + bi$, where a and b are real numbers and $i = \sqrt{-1}$.

a is called the **real part** of the complex number and b is called the **imaginary part** of the complex number.

(2) We can multiply two complex numbers by formally taking the product of two binomials and then replacing i^2 by -1.

$$(x + yi)(z + wi) = (xz - yw) + (xw + yz)i$$

In this question, we have $x = 0$, $y = 1$, $z = 1$, and $w = -3$.

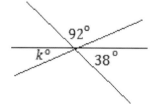

30. In the figure above, three lines intersect at a point. What is the value of k ?

(Lines and Angles)

* Let's use vertical angles to add some information to the picture.

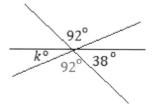

Now, observe that $k + 92 + 38 = 180$, so that $k = 180 - 92 - 38 = \mathbf{50}$.

Note: Two non-adjacent angles formed by two intersecting lines are called **vertical angles.** In the figure below, $\angle a$ and $\angle c$ form a pair of vertical angles, and $\angle b$ and $\angle d$ also form a pair of vertical angles.

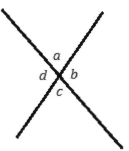

Vertical angles are **congruent**, meaning they have the same measure. For example, $m\angle a = m\angle c$. We can also write $\angle a \cong \angle c$. The symbol "$\cong$" can be read "is congruent to."

31. What is the radius of a circle whose area is 64π ?

(Circles)

* Algebraic solution: We use the area formula $A = \pi r^2$, and substitute 64π in for A.

$$A = \pi r^2$$
$$64\pi = \pi r^2$$
$$64 = r^2$$
$$8 = r$$

So, the radius of the circle is $r = \mathbf{8}$.

Notes: (1) A **circle** is a two-dimensional geometric figure formed of a curved line surrounding a center point, every point of the line being an equal distance from the center point. This distance is called the **radius** of the circle.

(2) The equation $r^2 = 64$ would normally have two solutions: $r = 8$ and $r = -8$. But the radius of a circle must be positive, and so we reject -8.

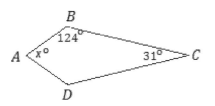

32. In the figure above, $AB = AD$ and $BC = DC$. What is the value of x ?

(Polygons)

* Since $AB = AD$ and $BC = DC$, the unlabeled angle inside the quadrilateral measures $124°$. It follows that $x = 360 - 124 - 124 - 31 = \mathbf{81}$.

Note: $ABCD$ is a quadrilateral. The angle measures of a quadrilateral sum to $360°$. It follows that $m\angle A + m\angle B + m\angle C + m\angle D = 360°$.

LEVEL 2: HEART OF ALGEBRA

$$9 + 3c \geq 8 + 3c$$

33. Which of the following best describes the solutions to the inequality above?

    A) $c \leq 1$
    B) $c \geq 1$
    C) All real numbers
    D) No solution

(Solving Linear Inequalities)

Solution by picking numbers: Let's try $c = 0$. The given inequality then becomes $9 \geq 8$, which is true. So, $c = 0$ is a solution to the inequality and we can eliminate choices B and D.

Let's try $c = 2$ next. The given inequality then becomes $9 + 3 \cdot 2 \geq 8 + 3 \cdot 2$, or equivalently, $15 \geq 14$, which is again true. So $c = 2$ is also a solution to the inequality and we can eliminate A.

It follows that the answer is choice **C**.

* Algebraic solution: We strike off $3c$ from each side to get $9 \geq 8$. Since this is true independent of the choice for c, every real number is a solution, choice **C**.

34. In the xy-plane, what is the x-intercept of the line with equation $y = 5x - 1$?

    A) $-\frac{1}{5}$
    B) 1
    C) $\frac{1}{5}$
    D) 5

(Equations of Lines and Their Graphs)

* We substitute 0 for y and solve for x. So, we have $0 = 5x - 1$. We add 1 to each side of this equation to get $1 = 5x$. Finally, we divide by 5 to get $x = \frac{1}{5}$, choice **C**.

Note: An **x-intercept** of a graph is a point on the graph where $y = 0$. An x-intercept has the form $(a, 0)$ for some real number a. Sometimes we may also say that the x-intercept is the number a.

We can find the x-intercept of the graph of an equation by setting $y = 0$ and solving for x.

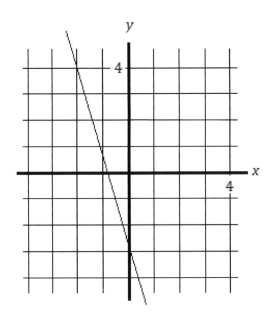

35. Which of the following is an equation of the line that is shown in the xy-plane above?

A) $y = -\frac{2}{7}x - 3$

B) $y = -\frac{7}{2}x - 3$

C) $y = \frac{2}{7}x + 3$

D) $y = \frac{7}{2}x - 3$

(Equations of Lines and Their Graphs)

* The line passes through the points $(-2, 4)$ and $(0, -3)$. It follows that the slope of the line is $m = \frac{-3-4}{0-(-2)} = \frac{-7}{2} = -\frac{7}{2}$. So, the answer must be choice **B**.

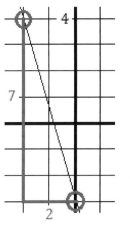

Notes: (1) We can also find the slope geometrically by observing that $\frac{\text{rise}}{\text{run}} = -\frac{7}{2}$. We can see this clearly in the picture on the right. Note that the slope is negative because we are going down and to the right.

(2) The y-intercept of the line is $b = -3$, as can clearly be seen on the given graph. It follows that the equation of the line in slope-intercept form is $y = -\frac{7}{2}x - 3$.

(3) See Problems 3 and 4 above for more information on slope and the slope-intercept form for the equation of a line.

Questions 36 - 37 refer to the following information.

A display case containing brass figurines is sitting on a shelf. The weight, in pounds, of the figurines together with the display case is given by the equation $W = 0.7f + 5$, where f is the number of figurines in the display case.

36. What is the best interpretation of the number 5 in the equation?

    A) The weight, in pounds, of the display case when it is empty
    B) The weight, in pounds, of the display case with 7 figurines inside of it
    C) The weight, in pounds, of 1 figurine
    D) The weight, in pounds, of 7 figurines

(Interpreting Linear Expressions)

* When $f = 0$, $W = 5$. This means that the weight of 0 figurines together with the display case is 5 pounds. Since there are 0 figurines, the display case is empty. So, the answer is choice **A**.

37. What is the best interpretation of the number 0.7 in the equation?

    A) The weight, in pounds, of the display case when it is empty
    B) The weight, in pounds, of the display case with 5 figurines inside of it
    C) The weight, in pounds, of 1 figurine
    D) The weight, in pounds, of 5 figurines

(Interpreting Linear Expressions)

* **Algebraic solution:** The equation is linear with a slope of 0.7. This means that an increase in f by 1 figurine corresponds to an increase in W by 0.7 pounds. So, every time we add a figurine to the display case, the total weight increases by 0.7 pounds. Therefore, each figurine weighs 0.7 pounds, and the answer is choice **C**.

Note: Recall that the slope of a line is

$$\text{Slope} = m = \frac{\text{change in the dependent variable}}{\text{change in the independent variable}} = \frac{\text{change in } W}{\text{change in } f}$$

Also recall that the **slope-intercept form of an equation of a line** is $y = mx + b$ where m is the slope of the line. In the given equation, $W = 0.7f + 5$, we use W and f instead of y and x. We see that the slope is $m = 0.7 = \frac{0.7}{1}$. So, a change in f by 1 unit corresponds to a change in W by 0.7 units. In other words, adding 1 figurine to the display case increases the total weight by 0.7 pounds.

Since the sign of 0.7 is positive ($0.7 = +0.7$), there is a **positive association** between f and W. It follows that an increase in f corresponds to an increase in W. So, if the number of figurines f is increased by 1, the total weight is increased by 0.7 pounds.

$$2x \le 3y + 1$$
$$x - y > 1$$

38. Which of the following ordered pairs (x, y) satisfies the system of inequalities above?

    A) $(0, 0)$
    B) $(0, -2)$
    C) $(2, -1)$
    D) $(6, 4)$

(Advanced Linear Systems)

* Solution by starting with choice C: We start with choice C, letting $x = 2$ and $y = -1$. We substitute these values into the first inequality giving us $2 \cdot 2 \leq 3(-1) + 1$, or equivalently, $4 \leq -2$. This is false, and so the point $(2, -1)$ does not satisfy the first inequality. So, we can eliminate choice C. Let's try choice D next and let $x = 6$ and $y = 4$. We substitute these values into the first inequality giving us $2 \cdot 6 \leq 3 \cdot 4 + 1$, or equivalently, $12 \leq 13$. This is true. Let's now substitute into the second inequality. We get $6 - 4 > 1$, or equivalently, $2 > 1$. This is also true, and so, the answer is choice **D**.

$$3(a + 1) - 7(a + b) = 2a - 7b$$

39. What value of a satisfies the equation above?

(Solving Linear Equations)

* Algebraic solution: We use the distributive property on the left: $3a + 3 - 7a - 7b = 2a - 7b$. We can now strike off $-7b$ from each side to get $3a + 3 - 7a = 2a$. Combining like terms on the left yields $-4a + 3 = 2a$. We add $4a$ to each side of this last equation to get $3 = 2a + 4a = 6a$. Finally, we divide by 6 to get $a = \frac{3}{6} = \mathbf{1/2}$ or $\mathbf{.5}$.

Note: See Problem 5 above for more information on the distributive property.

$$x - y = 7$$
$$x + y = 9$$

40. If (a, b) is the solution to the system of equations above, what is the value of b ?

(Solving Linear Systems of Equations)

* Solution using the elimination method: We replace x by a and y by b, and add the two equations.

$$\begin{array}{r} a - b = 7 \\ \underline{a + b = 9} \\ 2a \phantom{{} + b} = 16 \end{array}$$

So, $a = \frac{16}{2} = 8$. Substituting this value for a into the second equation gives us $8 + b = 9$. So, $b = \mathbf{1}$.

Notes: (1) We can get b right away (without finding a first) by subtracting the two equations instead. This may be a little riskier because a computational error is more likely. Here is how the computation might look.

$$\begin{array}{r} a - b = 7 \\ \underline{a + b = 9} \\ -2b = -2 \end{array}$$

So, $b = \frac{-2}{-2} = 1$.

(2) The answer to this question can be gotten very quickly by some simple reasoning. We're looking for two numbers whose difference is 7 and whose sum is 9. Since 8 is midway between 7 and 9, we have $8 - 1 = 7$ and $8 + 1 = 9$. So, $a = 8$ and $b = 1$.

LEVEL 2: PASSPORT TO ADVANCED MATH

41. For $x \neq 0$, which of the following is equivalent to $\dfrac{x^4 + x^2}{x^2}$?

        A) x^2
        B) $2x^2$
        C) $x^2 + 1$
        D) $x^2 + 2$

(Factoring)

*

$$\frac{x^4 + x^2}{x^2} = \frac{x^2(x^2 + 1)}{x^2} = x^2 + 1$$

This is choice **C**.

Note: $x^2(x^2 + 1) = x^2 \cdot x^2 + x^2 \cdot 1 = x^{2+2} + x^2 = x^4 + x^2$ (see Problem 5 and Problem 10).

42. If $g(x) = \dfrac{k}{x}$, where k is a constant, and $g(4) = 3$, then what is x when $g(x) = 6$?

(Functions)

Algebraic solution: We are given that $g(4) = 3$, and so, $3 = \dfrac{k}{4}$, or equivalently, $k = 12$. Therefore, $g(x) = \dfrac{12}{x}$. When $g(x) = 6$, we have $\dfrac{12}{x} = 6$, or equivalently, $12 = 6x$. So, $x = \dfrac{12}{6} = $ **2**.

Solution using inverse variation: Letting $y = g(x)$, we have $xy = k$, and so, we have $3 \cdot 4 = x \cdot 6$, or equivalently, $x = \dfrac{3 \cdot 4}{6} = \dfrac{12}{6} = $ **2**.

Note: The following are all equivalent ways of saying the same thing:

(1) y varies inversely as x.
(2) y is inversely proportional to x.
(3) $y = \dfrac{k}{x}$ for some constant k.
(4) xy is constant.

By (3), the expression $g(x) = \dfrac{k}{x}$ gives an inverse relationship between x and $g(x)$. By (4), this means that xy always gives the same value. $g(4) = 3$ means that when $x = 4$, $y = 3$. Similarly, $g(x) = 6$ means "what is x" when $y = 6$? So, $4 \cdot 3$ and $x \cdot 6$ have the same value.

* Quick solution: $x = \frac{3 \cdot 4}{6} = 2$.

43. Which of the following is equivalent to $(-3x^2y + 2xy^2) - (-3x^2y - 2xy^2)$?

   A) 0
   B) $4xy^2$
   C) $-6x^2y$
   D) $-6x^2y + 4xy^2$

(Operations on Polynomials)

* Algebraic solution:
$$(-3x^2y + 2xy^2) - (-3x^2y - 2xy^2)$$
$$= -3x^2y + 2xy^2 + 3x^2y + 2xy^2$$
$$= (-3x^2y + 3x^2y) + (2xy^2 + 2xy^2) = 0 + 4xy^2 = 4xy^2$$

This is choice **B**.

44. Which of the following expressions is equal to 0 for some value of x ?

   A) $|x - 0.5| + 0.1$
   B) $|x + 0.5| + 0.1$
   C) $|0.5 - x| - 0.1$
   D) $|0.5 - x| + 0.1$

(Manipulating Nonlinear Expressions)

* Since $|z| \geq 0$ for all z, $|z| + 0.1 \geq 0.1$ for all z. In particular, choices A, B, and D cannot be equal to 0. So, the answer is choice **C**.

Notes: (1) $|x|$ is the **absolute value** of x. If x is nonnegative, then $|x| = x$. If x is negative, then $|x| = -x$ (in other words, if x is negative, then taking the absolute value just eliminates the minus sign). For example, $|12| = 12$ and $|-12| = 12$. The absolute value of something is *always* greater than or equal to 0.

(2) Substituting $x = 0.4$ into choice C yields

$$|0.5 - x| - 0.1 = |0.5 - 0.4| - 0.1 = |0.1| - 0.1 = 0.1 - 0.1 = 0.$$

$x = 0.6$ would work as well.

45. If $(x - 3)^2 = 36$, and $x < 0$, what is the value of x ?

   A) -33
   B) -9
   C) -3
   D) -2

(Solving Quadratic Equations)

* Algebraic solution: We use the **square root property**, and then solve for x.

$$(x - 3)^2 = 36$$
$$x - 3 = \pm 6$$
$$x = 3 \pm 6$$
$$x = 3 - 6 \text{ or } x = 3 + 6$$
$$x = -3 \text{ or } x = 9$$

Since it is given that $x < 0$, the answer is $x = -3$, choice **C**.

Note: See Problem 12 for more information about the square root property.

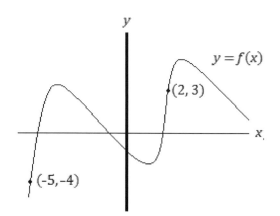

46. The figure above shows the graph of the function f in the xy-plane. What is the value of $f(2) - f(-5)$?

(Graphs of Functions)

* The points $(2, 3)$ and $(-5, -4)$ lie on the graph of the function f. Therefore, $f(2) = 3$ and $f(-5) = -4$. So, it follows that $f(2) - f(-5) = 3 - (-4) = 3 + 4 =$ **7**.

Note: If f is a function, then $f(a) = b$ is equivalent to "the point (a, b) lies on the graph of f."

47. If $\sqrt[3]{b^2} = b^k$, what is the value of k ?

(Exponents and Roots)

* $\sqrt[3]{b^2} = (b^2)^{\frac{1}{3}} = b^{\frac{2}{3}}$. So, $k =$ **2/3** or **.666**, or **.667**.

Notes: (1) For the first step, we used the law of exponents in the tenth row of the table (after Problem 10).

(2) For the second step, we used the law of exponents in the fifth row of the table (after Problem 10) to write $(b^2)^{\frac{1}{3}} = b^{2 \cdot \frac{1}{3}} = b^{\frac{2}{3}}$.

(3) We could have also taken just a single step by using row 11 in the table (after Problem 10) to write $\sqrt[3]{b^2} = b^{\frac{2}{3}}$.

$$3(-2x^3 - 3x + 2) - 5(x^3 - x^2 - 3x) = ax^3 + bx^2 + cx + d$$

48. In the equation above, a, b, c, and d are constants. If the equation is true for all values of x, what is the value of b ?

(Manipulating Nonlinear Expressions)

* Quick solution: Since b is the coefficient of x^2, we simply compute $-5(-x^2) = 5x^2$. It follows that $b = \mathbf{5}$.

Complete computation:
$$3(-2x^3 - 3x + 2) - 5(x^3 - x^2 - 3x)$$
$$= -6x^3 - 9x + 6 - 5x^3 + 5x^2 + 15x$$
$$= -11x^3 + 5x^2 + 6x + 6$$

So, we have $-11x^3 + 5x^2 + 6x + 6 = ax^3 + bx^2 + cx + d$.

It follows that $a = -11$, $b = 5$, $c = 6$, and $d = 6$.

In particular, $b = \mathbf{5}$.

LEVEL 2: PROBLEM SOLVING

49. * A recipe requires 3.5 ounces of red pepper per serving. How many pounds of red pepper are needed to make 60 servings? (1 pound = 16 ounces)

    A) 10.275
    B) 13.125
    C) 100.25
    D) 210

(Ratios)

Solution by setting up ratios: Key words: "ounces" and "servings"

ounces	3.5	x
servings	1	60

$$\frac{3.5}{1} = \frac{x}{60} \Rightarrow x = 3.5 \cdot 60 = 210$$

So, 210 ounces are needed to make 60 servings. We still need to change ounces to pounds.

Key words: "ounces" and "pounds"

ounces	210	16
pounds	x	1

$$\frac{210}{x} = \frac{16}{1} \Rightarrow 16x = 210 \Rightarrow x = \frac{210}{16} = 13.125$$

The answer is choice **B**.

* **Quick solution:** 60 servings require $3.5 \cdot 60 = 210$ ounces, and 210 ounces is $\frac{210}{16} = 13.125$ pounds, choice **B**.

Questions 50 - 51 refer to the following information.

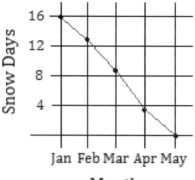

Month

The line graph above shows the average number of days that it snows at least 0.1 inch in Buffalo, NY from January to May.

50. According to the graph, the number of snow days in April is approximately what fraction of the number of snow days in February?

    A) $\frac{3}{13}$

    B) $\frac{11}{25}$

    C) $\frac{3}{5}$

    D) $\frac{13}{16}$

(Graphs)

* There are approximately 3 snow days in April and 13 snow days in February. So, the desired fraction is $\frac{3}{13}$, choice **A**.

51. According to the graph, approximately what was the least decrease in the number of snow days from one month to the next month?

    A) 2
    B) 3
    C) 4
    D) 6

(Graphs)

* The decrease from Jan to Feb is approximately $16 - 13 = 3$, choice **B**.

Note: The decrease from Apr to May is also approximately $3 - 0 = 3$.

The decrease from Feb to Mar is approximately $13 - 9 = 4$.

The decrease from Mar to Apr is approximately $9 - 3 = 6$.

52. If $y = kx$, where k a constant, and $y = 7$ when $x = 11$, then what is y when $x = 33$?

(Ratios)

Algebraic solution: We are given that $y = 7$ when $x = 11$, and so, $7 = k(11)$, or $k = \frac{7}{11}$. Therefore, $y = \frac{7x}{11}$. When $x = 33$, we have $y = \frac{7(33)}{11} = \mathbf{21}$.

Solution using direct variation: Since $y = kx$, y varies directly as x, and so $\frac{y}{x}$ is a constant. So, we get the following ratio: $\frac{7}{11} = \frac{y}{33}$. Cross multiplying gives $7 \cdot 33 = 11y$, so that $y = \frac{7 \cdot 33}{11} = \mathbf{21}$.

Graphical solution: The graph of $y = f(x)$ is a line passing through the points $(0, 0)$ and $(11, 7)$ The slope of this line is $\frac{7 - 0}{11 - 0} = \frac{7}{11}$. Writing the equation of the line in slope-intercept form we have $y = \frac{7}{11}x$. As in the algebraic solution above, when $x = 33$, we have $y = \frac{7(33)}{11} = \mathbf{21}$.

* Quick solution: To get from $x = 11$ to $x = 33$ we multiply x by 3. So, we have to also multiply y by 3. We get $3(7) = \mathbf{21}$.

Note: The following are all equivalent ways of saying the same thing:

(1) y varies directly as x.
(2) y is directly proportional to x.
(3) $y = kx$ for some constant k.
(4) $\frac{y}{x}$ is constant.
(5) The graph of $y = f(x)$ is a nonvertical line through the origin.

Questions 53 - 54 refer to the following information.

A survey was conducted among a randomly chosen sample of 150 males and 200 females to gather data on pet ownership. The data are shown in the table below.

	Has pets	Does not have pets	Total
Men	100	50	150
Women	56	144	200
Total	156	194	350

53. According to the table, what percent of the women surveyed do not have pets? (Disregard the percent symbol when gridding your answer.)

(Tables and Percents)

* There is a total of 200 women, and of these women, 144 do not have pets. So, the answer is $\frac{144}{200} \cdot 100 = \frac{144}{2} = 72\%$, and so, we grid in **72**.

Note: To compute a percentage, use the simple formula

$$\text{Percentage} = \frac{\text{Part}}{\text{Whole}} \times 100$$

In this example, the *Part* is the number of women who do not have pets and the *Whole* is the total number of women surveyed.

54. * According to the table, what is the probability that a randomly selected person with pets is female?

(Tables and Probability)

* There are 156 people who have pets, and of these, 56 are women. So, the desired probability is $56/156 \approx 0.35897$. So, we can grid in $.358$ or $.359$.

55. To increase the mean of 6 numbers by 5, by how much would the sum of the 6 numbers need to increase?

(Statistics)

Solution by picking numbers: Let's pick some numbers. The numbers 10, 10, 10, 10, 10, and 10 have a mean of 10 and a sum of 60. The numbers 15, 15, 15, 15, 15, and 15 have a mean of 15 and a sum of 90. So, to increase the mean by 5 we had to increase the sum by $90 - 60 = $ **30**.

* **Quick solution:** One way to increase the mean of a list of numbers by 5 is to increase **each** number in the list by 5. Since there are 6 numbers, the sum must be increased by $6 \cdot 5 = $ **30**.

56. 30 percent of 50 is 10 percent of what number?

(Percents)

Algebraic solution: We replace "percent" by "/100," we replace "of" by "·," we replace "is" by "=," we replace we replace "what" by x, and we solve the resulting equation for x.

$$\frac{30}{100} \cdot 50 = \frac{10}{100} \cdot x$$
$$30 \cdot 50 = 10x$$
$$x = \frac{30 \cdot 50}{10} = \mathbf{150}$$

* **Quick solution:** 30% of 50 is $0.3 \cdot 50 = 15$. So, if we let x be the number, then we have $15 = 0.1x$. So, $x = \frac{15}{0.1} = $ **150**.

Note: We change a percent to a decimal by moving the decimal point to the left 2 places. The number 30 has a "hidden" decimal point at the end of the number ($30 = 30.$ or 30.0). When we move this decimal point to the left two places we get $.30$ or 0.3.

LEVEL 2: GEOMETRY AND COMPLEX NUMBERS

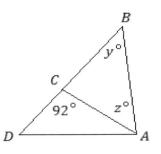

57. In $\triangle ABD$ above, if $z = 26$, what is the value of y?

    A) 26
    B) 66
    C) 88
    D) 92

(Lines, Angles, and Triangles)

TRIANGLE FACT 1: The measures of the interior angles of a triangle sum to 180°.

Solution using TRIANGLE FACT 1: The unlabeled angle in triangle ABC measures $180 - 92 = 88°$ degrees. So, $y = 180 - 26 - 88 = 66$, choice **B**.

TRIANGLE FACT 2: The measure of an exterior angle to a triangle is the sum of the measures of the two opposite interior angles of the triangle.

* **Solution using TRIANGLE FACT 2:** $92 = y + z = y + 26$. Thus, $y = 92 - 26 = 66$, choice **B**.

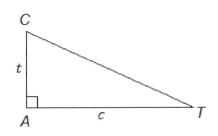

58. Given $\triangle CAT$ above, which of the following is equal to $\dfrac{t}{c}$?

    A) $\cos C$
    B) $\cos T$
    C) $\tan C$
    D) $\tan T$

(Trigonometry)

* Just note that $\tan T = \dfrac{\text{OPP}}{\text{ADJ}} = \dfrac{CA}{AT} = \dfrac{t}{c}$, choice **D**.

Note: See Problem 28 for a review of the trigonometry needed to solve this problem.

59. In a scale drawing of a rectangular garden, the length of the garden is 5 centimeters and the width of the garden is 7 centimeters. The length of the actual garden is L meters. Which of the following functions, P can be used to represent the perimeter, in meters, of the actual garden?

A) $P = L + \dfrac{7L}{5}$

B) $P = 2\left(L + \dfrac{7L}{5}\right)$

C) $P = 5L + 7L$

D) $P = 2(5L + 7L)$

(Polygons)

* We first need to use a ratio to find the width. We'll use the key words "length" and "width."

length	5	L
width	7	W

$$\frac{5}{7} = \frac{L}{W} \Rightarrow 5W = 7L \Rightarrow W = \frac{7L}{5}$$

Now, the perimeter is $P = 2(L + W) = 2(L + \dfrac{7L}{5})$, choice **B**.

Note: The perimeter of a rectangle is $P = 2l + 2w$, where l is the length of the rectangle and w is the width of the rectangle.

60. The expression $(2 - i^2) + (3i^2 - i)$ can be written as $a + bi$, where $i = \sqrt{-1}$. What is the value of a ?

A) -1

B) 0

C) 1

D) 2

(Complex Numbers)

* First note that $i^2 = \left(\sqrt{-1}\right)^2 = -1$, so that $-i^2 = -(-1) = 1$ and $3i^2 = 3(-1) = -3$. So, we have $(2 - i^2) + (3i^2 - i) = (2 + 1) + (-3 - i)) = 3 - 3 - i = 0 - i$.

Therefore, $a = 0$, choice **B**.

Notes: (1) See Problem 29 for more information on complex numbers.

(2) We add two complex numbers simply by adding their real parts, and then adding their imaginary parts.

$$(x + yi) + (z + wi) = (x + z) + (y + w)i$$

For example, $3 + (-3 - i) = (3 + 0i) + (-3 - i) = (3 - 3) + (0 - 1)i = 0 - i = -i$.

61. The measure of angle P is $\frac{25\pi}{36}$ radians greater than the measure of angle Q. How much greater is the measure of angle P than the measure of angle Q, in degrees? (Disregard the degree symbol when gridding your answer.)

(Circles)

Solution using a ratio: We can convert between degree measure and radian measure by using the following simple ratio:

$$\frac{\text{degree measure}}{180°} = \frac{\text{radian measure}}{\pi}$$

So, we have

$$\frac{x°}{180°} = \frac{\left(\frac{25\pi}{36}\right)}{\pi}$$

Therefore, $x\pi = 180\left(\frac{25\pi}{36}\right) = 125\pi$. So, $x = \frac{125\pi}{\pi} = \mathbf{125}$.

Quicker solution: We can convert from radians to degrees by multiplying the given angle by $\frac{180}{\pi}$. So, we get $\frac{25\pi}{36} \cdot \frac{180}{\pi} = \mathbf{125}$.

* Quickest solution: When converting from radians to degrees, if the angle has π in the numerator, we can simply replace π by 180. So, we get $\frac{25\pi}{36} = \frac{25(180)}{36} = \mathbf{125}$.

62. The volume of a right circular cylinder is 375π cubic centimeters. If the height is three times the base radius of the cylinder, what is the base <u>diameter</u> of the cylinder, in centimeters?

(Solid Geometry)

Solution by taking a guess: Let's start with a guess of $d = 6$. Then we have $r = 3$, so that $h = 9$ and $V = \pi r^2 h = \pi(3)^2(9) = 81\pi$, too small.

Let's try $d = 10$ next. Then $r = 5$, and so, $h = 15$ and $V = \pi r^2 h = \pi(5)^2(15) = 375\pi$. This is correct, and so the base diameter is **10**.

* Algebraic solution:

$$V = \pi r^2 h$$
$$375\pi = \pi r^2(3r)$$
$$125 = r^3$$
$$5 = r.$$

Since $r = 5$, we have $d = 2r = 2 \cdot 5 = \mathbf{10}$.

Note: (1) The volume of a cylinder with base radius r and height h is $\boldsymbol{V = \pi r^2 h}$.

(2) The diameter of a circle is twice the radius. That is, $\boldsymbol{d = 2r}$.

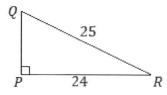

63. Triangle STU (not shown) is similar to triangle PQR, where vertices S, T, and U correspond to vertices P, Q, and R, respectively. If $SU = 12$, what is length of $\overline{ST}$?

(Parallel Lines and Similarity)

* We first use the Pythagorean triple 7, 24, 25 to get that $PQ = 7$. Then we have $\frac{ST}{SU} = \frac{PQ}{PR}$. Substituting the lengths that we know gives us $\frac{ST}{12} = \frac{7}{24}$. So, $ST = \frac{7}{24} \cdot 12 = \mathbf{7/2}$ or $\mathbf{3.5}$.

Notes: (1) The Pythagorean triple $7, 24, 25$ doesn't show up as much as the triples $3, 4, 5$ and $5, 12, 13$. If you do not remember this one, it's not a big deal. Just use the Pythagorean Theorem. The quick computation would like this:

$$PQ = \sqrt{25^2 - 24^2} = \sqrt{625 - 576} = \sqrt{49} = 7.$$

(2) Two triangles are **similar** if they have the same angle measures.

(3) Let's draw triangle STU next to triangle PQR. (this is always a good idea!)

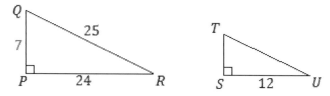

(4) **Corresponding sides of similar triangles are in proportion.** So, for example, in the figure we just drew, $\frac{ST}{SU} = \frac{PQ}{PR}$.

64. If $0 \le x \le 90°$ and $\cos x = \frac{5}{13}$, then $\tan x =$

(Trigonometry)

* **Trigonometric solution:** Let's draw a picture. We begin with a right triangle and label one of the angles x.

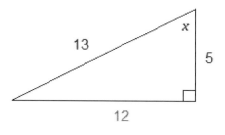

Since $\cos x = \frac{\text{ADJ}}{\text{HYP}}$, we label the leg adjacent to x with a 5 and the hypotenuse with 13. We can use the Pythagorean triple $5, 12, 13$ to see that the other side is 12.

Finally, $\tan x = \frac{\text{OPP}}{\text{ADJ}} = $ **12/5** or **2.4**.

Notes: (1) If you don't remember the Pythagorean triple $5, 12, 13$, you can use the Pythagorean Theorem:

Here we have $5^2 + b^2 = 13^2$. Therefore, $25 + b^2 = 169$. Subtracting 25 from each side of this equation gives $b^2 = 169 - 25 = 144$. So, $b = 12$.

We can also do this computation quickly as follows:
$$\sqrt{13^2 - 5^2} = \sqrt{169 - 25} = \sqrt{144} = 12$$

(2) The equation $b^2 = 144$ would normally have two solutions: $b = 12$ and $b = -12$. But the length of a side of a triangle cannot be negative, so we reject -12.

(3) See Problem 28 for a review of the trigonometry needed to solve this problem.

LEVEL 3: HEART OF ALGEBRA

65. A cell phone provider charges customers a one time setup fee of $40 plus k dollars for each month. If a customer paid $1120 for the first 12 months, including the setup fee, what is the value of k ?

A) 80
B) 90
C) 100
D) 110

(Solving Linear Equations)

* **Algebraic solution:** We are given that $12k + 40 = 1120$. Subtracting 40 from each side of this equation gives us $12k = 1120 - 40 = 1080$. Dividing each side of this last equation by 12 gives us $k = \frac{1080}{12} = 90$, choice **B**.

Notes: (1) A customer pays 40 dollars for 0 months.

A customer pays $k + 40$ dollars for 1 month.

A customer pays $2k + 40$ dollars for 2 months.

Following this pattern, a customer pays $12k + 40$ dollars for 12 months.

(2) This problem can also be solved by plugging in the answer choices. I leave the details to the reader.

66. Francisco brought $20 with him to school. At lunchtime, Francisco spent x dollars, and during another break, Francisco spent y dollars, leaving him with less than $7. Which of the following inequalities can be used to represent this situation?

    A) $7 - x - y < 20$
    B) $7 - x + y < 20$
    C) $20 - x - y < 7$
    D) $20 - x + y < 7$

(Setting Up Linear Expressions)

* Algebraic solution: Starting with $20, Francisco spent x dollars, and then y dollars. So, Francisco is left with $20 - x - y$ dollars. Since he was left with less than $7, we need the quantity $20 - x - y$ to be less than 7. This is written $20 - x - y < 7$, choice **C**.

Note: This problem can also be solved by picking numbers. I leave this solution to the reader.

$$\frac{1}{3}x - \frac{1}{6}y = 7$$
$$\frac{1}{5}y - \frac{1}{5}x = 8$$

67. Which of the following ordered pairs (x, y) satisfies the system of equations above?

    A) $(-36, -57)$
    B) $(12, 43)$
    C) $(\frac{101}{5}, \frac{307}{5})$
    D) $(82, 122)$

(Solving Linear Systems of Equations)

* Solution using the elimination method: Let's begin by multiplying the first equation by 6 and the second equation by 5 to get rid of the denominators. So, we have

$$2x - y = 42$$
$$y - x = 40$$

Let's rewrite $y - x$ as $-x + y$ and add the two equations.

$$2x - y = 42$$
$$\underline{-x + y = 40}$$
$$x = 82$$

Let's substitute $x = 82$ into the second equation in the solution to get $y - 82 = 40$. Adding 82 gives $y = 40 + 82 = 122$.

So, the answer is $(82, 122)$, choice **D**.

Solution by plugging in the points: Let's begin plugging the answer choices into the given equations.

Choice C looks to be difficult, so let's start with choice B.

$$\frac{1}{3}x - \frac{1}{6}y = \frac{1}{3}(12) - \frac{1}{6}(43) = 4 - \frac{43}{6} \neq 7$$

So, we can eliminate choice B.

Let's try D next.

$$\frac{1}{3}x - \frac{1}{6}y = \frac{1}{3}(82) - \frac{1}{6}(122) = \frac{2 \cdot 82}{6} - \frac{122}{6} = \frac{164 - 122}{6} = \frac{42}{6} = 7$$

$$\frac{1}{5}y - \frac{1}{5}x = \frac{1}{5}(122) - \frac{1}{5}(82) = \frac{122 - 82}{5} = \frac{40}{5} = 8$$

So, the answer is choice **D**.

68. The company *Hummus and More* sells hummus in 12-ounce and 16-ounce tubs. During one week, a supermarket sold 423 tubs of hummus, totaling 5820 ounces. Which of the following systems of equations could be used to determine the number of tubs of each size of hummus that was sold at the supermarket, where x is the number of 12-ounce tubs sold and y is the number of 16-ounce tubs sold?

A) $x + y = 5820$
   $28xy = 423$

B) $x + y = 423$
   $28xy = 5820$

C) $x + y = 5820$
   $12x + 16y = 423$

D) $x + y = 423$
   $12x + 16y = 5820$

(Setting Up Linear Systems)

* Since x is the number of 12-ounce tubs of hummus sold and y is the number of 16-ounce tubs of hummus sold, it follows that $x + y$ is the total number of tubs of hummus sold at the supermarket. We are given that the supermarket sold 423 tubs of hummus, and so $x + y = 423$. This narrows down the possible answers to choices B and D.

Now, $12x$ is the number of ounces of hummus sold in 12-ounce tubs, and $16y$ is the number of ounces of hummus sold in 16-ounce tubs. So, the total number of ounces of hummus sold at the supermarket was $12x + 16y$ We are told that the total number of ounces of hummus sold at the supermarket was 5820 ounces, and so $12x + 16y = 5820$. So, the answer is choice **D**.

69. When 9 times the number k is added to 24, the result is 42. What number results when 3 times k is added to 15 ?

(Solving Linear Equations)

Algebraic solution: We are given that $24 + 9k = 42$. Subtracting 24 from each side of this equation gives us $9k = 42 - 24 = 18$. Dividing each side of this last equation by 3 gives us $3k = 6$.

Finally, $15 + 3k = 15 + 6 = \textbf{21}$.

Notes: (1) 9 times the number k can be written as $9k$.

(2) 9 times the number k added to 24 can be rewritten as $9k$ added to 24. This is $24 + 9k$.

(3) Although writing "$9k$ added to 24" as $9k + 24$ will give the correct answer, it is not the correct interpretation (Note (2) shows how to write it correctly). Making this mistake when adding will not hurt you, but if you make this mistake when subtracting, you will get the wrong answer.

(3) "3 times k" can be written as $3k$.

(4) "3 times k added to 15" is "$3k$ added to 15" which is $15 + 3k$.

(5) in the solution above, we chose to divide each side of the equation $9k = 18$ by 3 instead of 9 because it saves us one algebraic step.

It wouldn't be wrong to divide by 9, but you would then have to multiply each side of the resulting equation by 3 afterwards.

70. The graph of the equation $5y - 7x = 11$ in the xy-plane intersects the y-axis at the point $(0, k)$. What is the value of k ?

(Equations of Lines and Their Graphs)

* We substitute 0 for x and k for y into the equation and solve for k. We get $5k - 7 \cdot 0 = 11$, or equivalently, $5k = 11$. Dividing each side of this last equation by 5 gives $k = \textbf{11/5}$ or $\textbf{2.2}$.

$$x - y = 2.2$$
$$5x + y = 1.4$$

71. If (x, y) satisfies the system of equations above, what is the value of x ?

(Solving Linear Systems of Equations)

* **Solution using the elimination method:** We add the two equations to get $6x = 3.6$. Dividing by 6 gives us $x = \frac{3.6}{6} = \textbf{.6}$ or $\textbf{3/5}$.

$$3k(2 - 5x) = 4 - 10x$$

72. In the equation above, k is a constant. If infinitely many values of x satisfy the equation, what is the value of k ?

(Advanced Linear Systems)

* We distribute on the left to get $6k - 15kx = 4 - 10x$. In order for there to be infinitely many solutions, the $x's$ must "go away." So, we need $-15k = -10$, or equivalently, $k = \frac{-10}{-15} = \textbf{2/3}$.

Notes: (1) We can also grid in $.\textbf{666}$ or $.\textbf{667}$.

(2) Observe that when we replace k by $\frac{2}{3}$ in the original equation, the left-hand side becomes $3 \cdot \frac{2}{3}(2 - 5x) = 2(2 - 5x) = 4 - 10x$, which is identical to the right-hand side. In other words, we have changed the equation into an *identity*, and the equation is true for all values of x.

Solution using a linear system: We can rewrite the given equation as the following system of linear equations.

$$y = 3k(2 - 5x)$$
$$y = 4 - 10x$$

We can distribute on the right-hand side of the first equation to get $y = 6k - 15kx$, and we can then rewrite each equation in general form.

$$15kx + y = 6k$$
$$10x + y = 4$$

For this system to have infinitely many solutions, we need $\frac{15k}{10} = \frac{1}{1} = \frac{6k}{4}$. Using the first part $\frac{15k}{10} = \frac{1}{1}$, we cross multiply to get $15k = 10$, and then divide to get $k = \frac{10}{15} = \mathbf{2/3}$.

Notes: (1) The **general form of an equation of a line** is $\boldsymbol{ax + by = c}$, where a, b, and c are real numbers. If $b \neq 0$, then the slope of this line is $m = -\frac{a}{b}$. If $b = 0$, then the line is vertical and has no slope. Let us consider 2 such equations.

$$\boldsymbol{ax + by = c}$$
$$\boldsymbol{dx + ey = f}$$

If there is a number r such that $ra = d$, $rb = e$, and $rc = f$, then the two equations represent the **same line**. Equivalently, the two equations represent the same line if $\frac{a}{d} = \frac{b}{e} = \frac{c}{f}$. In this case, the system of equations has **infinitely many solutions**.

If there is a number r such that $ra = d$, $rb = e$, but $rc \neq f$, then the two equations represent **parallel** but distinct lines. Equivalently, the two equations represent parallel but distinct lines if $\frac{a}{d} = \frac{b}{e} \neq \frac{c}{f}$. In this case the system of equations has **no solution**.

Otherwise the two lines intersect in a single point. In this case $\frac{a}{d} \neq \frac{b}{e}$, and the system of equations has a **unique solution**.

These three cases are illustrated in the figure below.

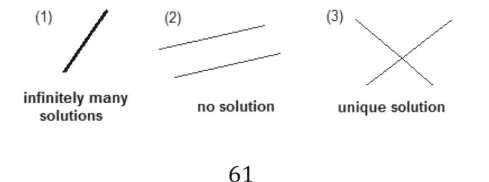

(1) infinitely many solutions

(2) no solution

(3) unique solution

(2) We can check that $\frac{6k}{4} = \frac{6\left(\frac{2}{3}\right)}{4} = \frac{4}{4} = 1$. Since all 3 fractions are equal to 1 when we replace k by $\frac{2}{3}$, we get a system with infinitely many solutions.

(3) If the last equation were not equal to 1, we would have no solution instead of infinitely many.

LEVEL 3: PASSPORT TO ADVANCED MATH

$$ax^4 + bx^3 + cx^2 + dx + e = 0$$

73. In the equation above, a, b, c, d, and e are constants, and -3, -1, 0, and 4 are roots of the equation. Which of the following is a factor of $ax^4 + bx^3 + cx^2 + dx + e$?

    A) $x - 4$
    B) $x - 3$
    C) $x - 1$
    D) $x + 4$

(Factoring)

* Solution using the factor theorem: The factors of the polynomial equation are $x + 3$, $x + 1$, x, and $x - 4$. Of these, only $x - 4$ is an answer choice. So, the answer is choice **A**.

Notes: (1) A number r is a **root** (or **zero**, or **solution**) of a function p if $p(r) = 0$.

(2) The **factor theorem** says that r is a root of the polynomial $p(x)$ if and only if $x - r$ is a factor of the polynomial. For example, if 4 is a root of a polynomial, then $x - 4$ is a factor of the polynomial.

Questions 74 - 76 refer to the following information.

The entire graph of the function g is shown in the xy-plane below.

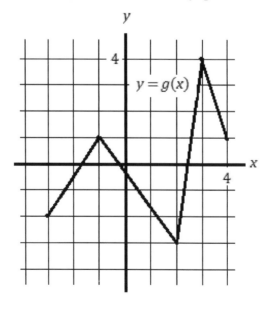

74. For what value of x is the value of $g(x)$ at its minimum?

    A) -3
    B) -2
    C) 2
    D) 4

(Graphs of Functions)

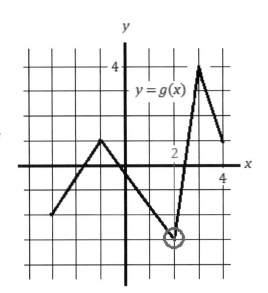

* Let's circle the minimum on the graph and observe that the minimum occurs at $x = 2$, choice **C**.

75. What is the minimum value of g ?

    A) -3
    B) -2
    C) 2
    D) 4

(Graphs of Functions)

* If we look at the graph in the solution to the previous problem, we see that the minimum value is $y = -3$, choice **A**.

Note: The minimum is always a y value. In this case, the minimum value is $y = -3$ and the minimum value occurs at $x = 2$.

76. On which of the following intervals is the graph of g increasing then decreasing?

    A) $-3 < x < 0$
    B) $0 < x < 2$
    C) $2 < x < 3$
    D) $3 < x < 4$

(Graphs of Functions)

* The graph of g is increasing from -3 to -1, and then decreasing from -1 to 0. So, from -3 to 0, the graph of g is increasing, then decreasing, choice **A**.

Note: From 0 to 2, the graph of g is decreasing.

From 2 to 3, the graph of g is increasing.

From 3 to 4, the graph of g is decreasing.

77. Which of the following is equivalent to $5^{-\frac{1}{2}}$?

    A) $-\sqrt{5}$

    B) $-\frac{1}{\sqrt{5}}$

    C) $\frac{1}{\sqrt{5}}$

    D) $\frac{1}{5^2}$

(Exponents and Roots)

* Solution using laws of exponents:

$$5^{-\frac{1}{2}} = \frac{1}{5^{\frac{1}{2}}} = \frac{1}{\sqrt{5}}$$

This is choice **C**.

Notes: (1) For the first step, we used the law of exponents in the ninth row of the table (after Problem 10) to write $5^{-\frac{1}{2}} = \frac{1}{5^{\frac{1}{2}}}$.

(2) For the second step, we used the law of exponents in the tenth row of the table (after Problem 10) to write $5^{\frac{1}{2}} = \sqrt{5}$.

$$X = \frac{3+y}{6} \qquad\qquad X = \frac{\sqrt{2y}}{2}$$

78. If the two formulas shown above are used to estimate the same quantity X, which of the following expressions is equivalent to $\sqrt{2y}$?

    A) $\frac{3+y}{6}$

    B) $\frac{3+y}{3}$

    C) $3 + y$

    D) $3(3 + y)$

(Manipulating Nonlinear Expressions)

* Since X is equal to both $\frac{3+y}{6}$ and $\frac{\sqrt{2y}}{2}$, we have $\frac{3+y}{6} = \frac{\sqrt{2y}}{2}$. We multiply each side of this equation by 2 to get $\sqrt{2y} = 2 \cdot \frac{3+y}{6} = \frac{3+y}{3}$, choice **B**.

$$\sqrt{3x - 5} = x - 1$$

79. What is the solution set of the equation above?

    A) $\{2\}$
    B) $\{3\}$
    C) $\{2, 3\}$
    D) There are no solutions.

(Solving Quadratic Equations)

Solution by starting with choice C: Let's start with choice C and guess that the answer is $\{2, 3\}$. We begin by substituting 2 for x into the given equation to get the equation $\sqrt{3 \cdot 2 - 5} = 2 - 1$. This is equivalent to $\sqrt{6 - 5} = 1$, or $1 = 1$. This is true!

Let's now substitute 3 for x into the given equation. We get $\sqrt{3 \cdot 3 - 5} = 3 - 1$. This is equivalent to $\sqrt{9 - 5} = 2$, or $2 = 2$. This is also true!

So, the answer is choice **C**.

$$h = -3t^2 + 5t$$

80. The equation above expresses the approximate height h, in meters, of a rock t seconds after it is thrown into the air with an initial velocity of 5 meters per second. After how many seconds will the rock hit the ground?

(Solving Quadratic Equations)

* The rock hits the ground when the height of the rock is 0. So, we set $h = 0$, or equivalently, $-3t^2 + 5t = 0$.

We now solve for t.

$$-3t^2 + 5t = 0$$
$$t(-3t + 5) = 0$$
$$t = 0 \quad \text{or} \quad -3t + 5 = 0$$
$$t = 0 \quad \text{or} \quad -3t = -5$$
$$t = 0 \quad \text{or} \quad t = \frac{-5}{-3} = \frac{5}{3}$$

So, we can grid in **5/3**, **1.66** or **1.67**.

Notes: (1) Although $t = 0$ is a solution to the equation $-3t^2 + 5 = 0$, it is not an acceptable answer because the rock was thrown at time $t = 0$, whereas we are looking for when the rock hit the ground (after it was thrown). Clearly, the rock hits the ground after time 0.

(2) Based on Note (1), after factoring, we can disregard the equation $t = 0$ and simply solve the equation $-3t + 5 = 0$.

LEVEL 3: PROBLEM SOLVING

81. A patch of ocean containing a single island has a total area of 536 square miles. The area of the water that does not include the island is 412 square miles. The total population of the island is currently 451,000 people. Assuming that the island comprises the total land mass in the given patch of ocean, which of the following is closest to the population density, in people per square mile of land area, of the island?

A) 840
B) 1100
C) 3650
D) 7000

(Ratios)

* The area of the island is $536 - 412 = 124$ square miles. Therefore, the population density is $\frac{451,000}{124} \approx 3637.1$. This is closest to 3650, choice **C**.

Questions 82 - 83 refer to the following information.

	Anxiety	No Anxiety	Total
Anxiety Medication	85	165	250
Placebo	115	135	250
Total	200	300	500

The table above shows the results of a controlled experiment that is being used to determine the effectiveness of an anxiety medication. A random sample of 500 adults received either the anxiety medication or a placebo each day during a 1 month time period. The adults reported whether they had anxiety during that time period.

82. According to the table, what proportion of adults who received the anxiety medication reported having anxiety during the 1 month time period?

A) $\frac{17}{100}$
B) $\frac{17}{50}$
C) $\frac{17}{30}$
D) $\frac{4}{5}$

(Tables)

* 250 of the adults received the anxiety medication, and of those adults, 85 of them reported having anxiety. So, the desired proportion is $\frac{85}{250} = \frac{17}{50}$, choice **B**.

83. According to the table, what is the probability that a randomly selected person with anxiety was given the placebo?

A) $\frac{17}{50}$

B) $\frac{17}{40}$

C) $\frac{23}{40}$

D) $\frac{17}{23}$

(Tables and Probability)

* There are 200 people with anxiety, and of these, 115 were given the placebo. So, the desired probability is $\frac{115}{200} = \frac{23}{40}$, choice **C**.

84. * Of the 400 juniors in Keyton high school, 48% scored higher than 1000 on the PSAT. Keyton high school is part of a school district with 7 high schools and the average size of the junior class for all 7 schools in the district is 400. If the students in Keyton high school are representative of students throughout the district, which of the following best estimates the number of high school juniors in the district who scored higher than 1000 on the PSAT?

A) 1100
B) 1350
C) 1500
D) 162

(Data Analysis)

* $0.48 \cdot 2800 = 1344$. This is closest to 1350, choice **B**.

85. A survey was given to a random sample of 100 guitar players in Alabama. The results of this survey should be representative of which of the following populations?

A) All musicians in the United States.
B) All musicians in Alabama
C) All guitar players in the United States
D) All guitar players in Alabama.

(Data Analysis)

* The results of the survey can be generalized to the population that the sample was drawn from. In this case, that is guitar players from Alabama, choice **D**.

Note: Don't change the population. The results from one population DO NOT carry over to another population.

In this problem, since the survey was given only to guitar players in Alabama, the result can be generalized only to the population of guitar players in Alabama.

Fat and Sugar for Ten Desserts

86. The scatterplot above shows the number of grams of fat and sugar for ten desserts. The line of best fit has been drawn. According to the line of best fit, which of the following is closest to the predicted decrease in sugar, in grams, for each increase of 1 gram of fat?

    A) 0.1
    B) 0.4
    C) 2.5
    D) 10

(Scatterplots)

* We are being asked to estimate the slope of the line of best fit. Two approximations to points on the line are $(5, 25)$ and $(30, 14)$. So, the slope is approximately $\frac{14-25}{30-5} = \frac{-11}{25} = -0.44$. The minus sign tells us that the line is decreasing. So, the predicted decrease is 0.44. This is closest to 0.4, choice **B**.

Note: Recall that the slope of a line is

$$\text{Slope} = m = \frac{\text{rise}}{\text{run}} = \frac{\text{change in vertical distance}}{\text{change in horizontal distance}}$$

In this problem, the change in vertical distance is the decrease in sugar, in grams, and the change in horizontal distance is the increase in fat, in grams.

Questions 87 - 88 refer to the following information.

A corporate note worth $1200 was purchased at the beginning of the year and since then it has lost 12% of its value each month. The equation $A = 1200(r)^t$ can be used to model the value, A, of the note t months from the beginning of the year.

87. What is the value of r in the expression?

(Growth)

* $r = 1 - 0.12 = \mathbf{0.88}$.

Notes: (1) We can also find the value of r by picking a number as follows: After 1 month, the note lost 12% of its value. So, if we let $t = 1$, then $A = 0.88 \cdot 1200 = 1056$. Therefore, we have $1056 = 1200(r)^1 = 1200r$. So, $r = \frac{1056}{1200} = .88$.

(2) To take away 12% is the same as taking 88%. Indeed, $100 - 12 = 88$. So, we can find A when $t = 1$ by multiplying 0.88 by 1200 to get 1056.

(3) We can also take 12% away from 1200 by first computing 12% of 1200, and then subtracting the result from 1200.

$$0.12 \cdot 1200 = 144$$
$$1200 - 144 = 1056$$

88. * If it is now 6 months since the note was purchased, to the nearest dollar, what is the note worth?

(Growth)

* From the last question, $r = 0.88$. It follows that $A = 1200(0.88)^6 \approx 557.2849$. To the nearest dollar this is **557**.

LEVEL 3: GEOMETRY AND COMPLEX NUMBERS

$$A \quad x \quad C \qquad 2y \qquad D \qquad 3z \qquad B$$

89. In the figure above, $AB = 99$. If $x = \frac{1}{3}y$ and $z = \frac{2}{3}x$, what is the length of line segment $\overline{DB}$?

   A) 11
   B) 22
   C) 33
   D) 35

(Lines and Angles)

* $y = 3x$, so that $2y = 6x$. We also have $3z = 3 \cdot \frac{2}{3}x = 2x$. So, $x + 2y + 3z = x + 6x + 2x = 9x$. Therefore, $9x = 99$, and so, $x = 11$. It follows that $\overline{DB} = 3z = 2x = 22$, choice **B**.

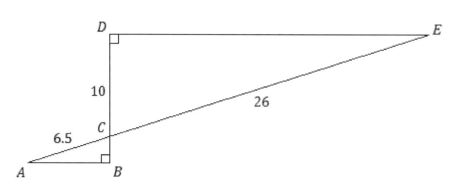

90. In the figure above, what is the length of $\overline{AB}$?

    A) 1.5
    B) 3
    C) 4
    D) 6

(Parallel Lines and Similarity)

* Using the Pythagorean triple $5, 12, 13$, we have $DE = 2 \cdot 12 = 24$. Now, $\triangle ABC \sim \triangle EDC$, and therefore, $\frac{AB}{AC} = \frac{DE}{CE}$. So, $\frac{AB}{6.5} = \frac{24}{26} = \frac{12}{13}$. Therefore, $AB = \frac{12}{13} \cdot 6.5 = 6$, choice **D**.

Notes: (1) See Problem 26 for more information on Pythagorean triples. A multiple of a Pythagorean triple is also a Pythagorean triple. Since 5, 12, 13 is a Pythagorean triple, so is 10, 24, 26.

(2) The symbol $\sim$ stands for "similar," so that $\triangle ABC \sim \triangle EDC$ is read "triangle ABC is similar to triangle EDC."

Recall from Problem 63 that two triangles are **similar** if they have the same angle measures.

(3) In this problem, $\angle ACB$ and $\angle ECD$ are **vertical angles**. Since vertical angles have the same measure, $m\angle ACB = m\angle ECD$.

Since angles B and D are both right angles, they are also congruent.

It follows that $\triangle ACB \sim \triangle ECD$.

(4) Corresponding sides of similar triangles are in proportion. So, for example, in this problem, we have $\frac{AB}{AC} = \frac{DE}{CE}$.

91. If k is a positive integer, then i^{4k+3} must be equal to which of the following?

    A) 1
    B) -1
    C) i
    D) $-i$

(Complex Numbers)

* $i^{4k+3} = i^{4k} \cdot i^3 = (i^4)^k \cdot i^3 = 1^k \cdot i^3 = 1 \cdot i^3 = i^3 = i^2 \cdot i = (-1)i = -i$, choice **D**.

Notes: (1) Since $i = \sqrt{-1}$, we have the following:

$$i^2 = \sqrt{-1}\,\sqrt{-1} = -1$$
$$i^3 = i^2 i = -1i = -i$$
$$i^4 = i^2 i^2 = (-1)(-1) = 1$$
$$i^5 = i^4 i = 1i = i$$

Notice that the pattern begins to repeat.

Starting with $i^0 = 1$, we have

$i^0 = 1$	$i^1 = i$	$i^2 = -1$	$i^3 = -i$
$i^4 = 1$	$i^5 = i$	$i^6 = -1$	$i^7 = -i$
$i^8 = 1$	$i^9 = i$	$i^{10} = -1$	$i^{11} = -i$

...

In other words, when we raise i to a nonnegative integer, there are only four possible answers:

$$1, i, -1, \text{or} -i$$

To decide which of these values is correct, we find the remainder upon dividing the exponent by 4.

* **Quick solution:** If k is an integer, then the expression $4k$ represents an integer that is divisible by 4. Similarly, $4k + 1$ represents an integer that gives a remainder of 1 when divided by 4, $4k + 2$ represents an integer that gives a remainder of 2 when divided by 4, and $4k + 3$ represents an integer that gives a remainder of 3 when divided by 4.

It follows that $i^{4k} = 1$, $i^{4k+1} = i$, $i^{4k+2} = -1$, and $i^{4k+3} = -i$, choice **D**.

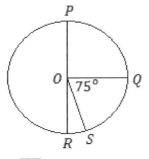

92. In the circle above with center O, $\overline{PR}$ is a diameter, $m\angle QOS = 75°$, and $\overline{OQ}$ and $\overline{OS}$ are radii. If the length of arc $\widehat{QS}$ is 10π, what is the length of $\overline{PR}$?

(Circles)

* **Solution by setting up a ratio:** We can set up a ratio to find the circumference of the circle.

arc	10π	C
degrees	75	360

71

$$\frac{10\pi}{75} = \frac{C}{360} \Rightarrow 75C = 3600\pi \Rightarrow C = \frac{3600\pi}{75} = 48\pi$$

Since the circumference of the circle is 48π, the diameter is **48**.

Solution using a formula: We can also use the formula $s = r\theta$ to find the radius of the circle. In this formula, r is the radius, θ is an angle in radians, and s is the length of the arc that the angle intercepts. So, in this problem, we have $s = 10\pi$ and $\theta = \frac{75\pi}{180} = \frac{5\pi}{12}$. So, using $s = r\theta$, we have $10\pi = r \cdot \frac{5\pi}{12}$, and therefore, $r = 10\pi \cdot \frac{12}{5\pi} = 24$. Finally, the diameter is $d = 2r = 2 \cdot 24 = $ **48**.

Note: See Problem 61 to learn how to set up the ratio for converting between radians and degrees. We can also convert from degrees to radians more quickly simply by multiplying the angle measure in degrees by $\frac{\pi}{180}$. So, to convert 75° into radians we multiply 75 by $\frac{\pi}{180}$ to get $\frac{75\pi}{180} = \frac{5\pi}{12}$.

93. A sugar wafer in the shape of a right circular cone has a height of 5 inches and contains enough liquid to fill half the volume of the cone. If the volume of liquid in the cone is $\frac{15\pi}{8}$ cubic inches, what is the diameter, in inches, of the base of the cone?

(Solid Geometry)

* Since the volume of the liquid in the cone is $\frac{15\pi}{8}$ cubic inches, the cone has a volume of $\frac{2}{1} \cdot \frac{15\pi}{8} = \frac{15\pi}{4}$ cubic inches. We use the formula for the volume of a cone: $V = \frac{1}{3}\pi r^2 h$

$$V = \frac{1}{3}\pi r^2 h \Rightarrow \frac{15\pi}{4} = \frac{1}{3}\pi r^2 \cdot 5 \Rightarrow r^2 = \frac{15\pi}{4} \cdot \frac{3}{5\pi} = \frac{3 \cdot 15}{4 \cdot 5} = \frac{9}{4} \Rightarrow r = \frac{3}{2} \Rightarrow d = 2r = 2 \cdot \frac{3}{2} = \textbf{3}$$

94. In a right triangle, one angle measures $x°$, where $\sin x° = \frac{3}{8}$. What is $\cos((90-x)°)$

(Trigonometry)

* **Solution using a cofunction identity:** $\cos((90-x)°) = \sin x° = \textbf{3/8} \text{ or } \textbf{.375}$.

Note: It's worth memorizing the following two cofunction identities for the SAT:

$$\sin(90° - x) = \cos x \qquad\qquad \cos(90° - x) = \sin x$$

Basic trig solution: Let's draw a picture:

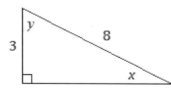

Notice that we labeled one of the angles with x, and used the fact that $\sin x = \frac{\text{OPP}}{\text{HYP}}$ to label two sides of the triangle.

Now observe that $y° = (90-x)°$, so that $\cos((90-\theta)°) = \cos y° = \frac{\text{ADJ}}{\text{HYP}} = \textbf{3/8} \text{ or } \textbf{.375}$.

Note: In the above solution, OPP stands for "opposite" and HYP stands for "hypotenuse." See Problem 28 for a review of the trigonometry used here.

95. A piece of string is formed into the shape of a regular hexagon, and another piece of string of equal length to the first piece of string is formed into the shape of a regular octagon. If each side of the hexagon is 5 centimeters longer than each side of the octagon, how long, in centimeters, is each piece of string?

(Polygons)

* Let x be the length of the string, in centimeters. The length of each side of the hexagon is then $\frac{x}{6}$ and the length of each side of the octagon is $\frac{x}{8}$. We are given that $\frac{x}{6} = \frac{x}{8} + 5$. If we multiply each side of this equation by 24, we get $4x = 3x + 120$. So, $x = \mathbf{120}$.

96. What is the radius of the circle in the xy-plane that has $(2, 7)$ as its center, and contains the point $(-10, 2)$?

(Graphs of Circles)

* Using the center of the circle, we can write the equation of the circle in standard form as

$$(x - 2)^2 + (y - 7)^2 = r^2$$

We can now find r by substituting -10 for x and 2 for y into this equation. We get

$$r^2 = (-10 - 2)^2 + (2 - 7)^2 = (-12)^2 + (-5)^2 = 144 + 25 = 169.$$

It follows that $r = \sqrt{169} = \mathbf{13}$.

Notes: (1) The equation of a circle in standard form is $(x - h)^2 + (y - k)^2 = r^2$, where (h, k) is the center of the circle and r is the radius of the circle. In this problem, we have $h = 2$ and $k = 7$.

(2) The radius of a circle is the distance between the center of the circle and any point on the circle. Therefore, we can also solve this problem by using the distance formula (which is basically the same as the equation of a circle in standard form) or by plotting the two points, drawing a right triangle and using the Pythagorean Theorem. See the solutions to Problem 127 in Problem Set B for details.

LEVEL 4: HEART OF ALGEBRA

97. A group of friends will be taking a road trip and they need to rent a car. *Discount Car Rentals* charges $50 per day plus $0.50 per mile driven, while *Rent-a-Cheap-Car* charges $80 per day with no additional charges for mileage. The group of friends will need the car for 7 days and they will drive a total of m miles. Which of the following inequalities gives all values of m for which the total charge of renting from *Discount Car Rentals* will be no more than the total charge of renting from *Rent-a-Cheap-Car*?

 A) $m \leq 60$
 B) $m \leq 210$
 C) $m \leq 420$
 D) $m \leq 840$

(Solving Linear Inequalities)

* Algebraic solution: The total cost for renting a car from Discount Car Rentals, in dollars, and driving m miles for 7 days is $7 \cdot 50 + 0.50m = 350 + 0.50m$. Similarly, the total cost for renting a car from Rent-a-Cheap-Car, in dollars, and driving m miles for 7 days is $7 \cdot 80 = 560$. We want to have $350 + 0.50m \leq 560$. We subtract 350 from each side of this inequality to get $0.50m \leq 210$. We now multiply each side of this last inequality by 2 to get $m \leq 420$, choice **C**.

98. To rent a bike, *Guiding Light Bike Rentals* charges $15 for the first hour and $4 for each additional hour. Which of the following gives the cost, $C(x)$, in dollars, of renting a bike for t hours?

 A) $C(t) = 19t$
 B) $C(t) = 15t + 4$
 C) $C(t) = 11t + 4$
 D) $C(t) = 4t + 11$

(Setting Up Linear Expressions)

Solution by picking numbers: Let's let $t = 3$, so that we are renting a bike for 3 hours. It then costs $15 for the first hour, $4 for the second hour, and $4 for the third hour. The total is $15 + 4 + 4 = \boxed{23}$ dollars. Let's now substitute $t = 3$ into each answer choice.

 A) $19 \cdot 3 = 57$
 B) $15 \cdot 3 + 4 = 45 + 4 = 49$
 C) $11 \cdot 3 + 4 = 33 + 4 = 37$
 D) $4 \cdot 3 + 11 = 12 + 11 = 23$

Since choices A, B, and C came out false, the answer is choice **D**.

* Algebraic solution: This is just a little bit tricky. At first glance, it might seem that the answer should be $C(t) = 4t + 15$. However, we need to analyze this problem a bit more carefully than other ones that look similar. If we were paying a fixed fee of \$15 plus another fee of \$4 per hour (including the first hour), then this would be correct. But that is not exactly what is going on here. We are only paying \$4 an hour starting from the *second* hour. So, if we want to think of \$15 as a fixed fee, then we have to adjust our t value accordingly. We can do this by replacing t by $t - 1$, so that we get $C(t) = 4(t - 1) + 15 = 4t - 4 + 15 = 4t + 11$. This is choice **D**.

Notes: (1) If a bike is rented for 1 hour, the cost is $C(1) = 15 = 4 \cdot 1 + 11$ dollars.

If a bike is rented for 2 hours, the cost is $C(2) = 15 + 4 = 19 = 4 \cdot 2 + 11$ dollars.

If a bike is rented for 3 hours, the cost is $C(3) = 15 + 4 + 4 = 23 = 4 \cdot 3 + 11$ dollars.

Following this pattern, we see that $C(t) = 4t + 11$.

(2) We can split up the first hour into \$4 and \$11. In this way, we can reframe the problem as having a fixed cost of \$11 and a variable cost of \$4 per hour. This time we are paying \$4 for the first hour, and so the problem is a bit more straightforward. As usual, we get $C(t) = 4t + 11$. Here $4t$ is the variable cost and 11 is the fixed cost.

99. In the xy-plane, line k has a slope of $-\frac{5}{3}$ and passes through the point $(6, -2)$. Which of the following is an equation of line k ?

    A) $y = 6x - \frac{5}{3}$
    B) $y = -\frac{5}{3}x - \frac{2}{3}$
    C) $y = -\frac{5}{3}x + 8$
    D) $y = -\frac{5}{3}x - 8$

(Equations of Lines and Their Graphs)

* We write an equation of the line in point-slope form as $y + 2 = -\frac{5}{3}(x - 6)$. Distributing on the right gives us $y + 2 = -\frac{5}{3}x + 10$. Finally, we subtract 2 from each side of this last equation to get $y = -\frac{5}{3}x + 8$, choice **C**.

Note: The point-slope form of an equation of a line is $y - y_0 = m(x - x_0)$, where m is the slope of the line and (x_0, y_0) is any point on the line.

In this problem, $m = -\frac{5}{3}$, $x_0 = 6$, and $y_0 = -2$. So, we get $y - (-2) = -\frac{5}{3}(x - 6)$. This can be simplified to $y + 2 = -\frac{5}{3}(x - 6)$.

$$F = 23{,}200 - 21k$$

100. The equation above estimates the total number of fish in a lake, F, in <u>hundreds</u>, in the kth year after the year 1995. The number 21 in the equation above gives which of the following estimates?

    A) Every 21 years, there are 232 fewer fish.
    B) Every 21 years, there are 23,200 fewer fish.
    C) Every year the total number of fish in the lake decreases by 21.
    D) Every year the total number of fish in the lake decreases by 2,100.

(Interpreting Linear Expressions)

* The given equation is linear with slope $-21 = \frac{-21}{1}$. This means that an increase in k by 1 unit corresponds to a decrease in F by 21 units. In other words, whenever the year is increased by 1, the number of fish in the lake decreases by $21 \cdot 100 = 2{,}100$, choice **D**.

Notes: (1) In the equation $F = 23{,}200 - 21k$, we are thinking of k as the **independent variable**, and F as the **dependent variable**. In other words, we input a value for k, and we get an F value as an output.

For example, if the input is $k = 2$ years after 1995, the output is $F = 23{,}200 - 21 \cdot 2 = 23{,}158$. Since F is given in hundreds, we need to multiply this last number by 100 to get the number of fish in 1997. So, in 1997, there were 2,315,800 fish in the lake.

(2) Recall that the slope of a line is

$$\text{Slope} = m = \frac{\text{change in the dependent variable}}{\text{change in the independent variable}} = \frac{\text{change in } F}{\text{change in } k}$$

(3) Also recall from Lesson 17 that the **slope-intercept form of an equation of a line** is $y = mx + b$ where m is the slope of the line. The given equation can be written $F = -21k + 23{,}200$, and we see that the slope is $m = -21 = \frac{-21}{1}$.

(4) Combining Notes (2) and (3), we see that a change in k by 1 unit corresponds to a change in F by 21 units.

(5) Since the sign of 21 is negative, there is a **negative association** between k and F. It follows that an increase in k corresponds to a decrease in F.

(6) Be certain to notice the underlined word <u>hundreds</u> in the question. If this wasn't there, the answer would be choice C. In this case however, when we substitute in a value for k, the corresponding F value needs to be multiplied by 100.

(7) When $k = 0$, $F = 23{,}200$. It follows that in 1995 there were 2,320,000 fish in the lake.

When $k = 1$, $F = 23{,}200 - 21 = 23{,}179$. It follows that in 1996 there were 2,317,900 fish in the lake.

From 1995 to 1996, the number of fish changed by $2{,}320{,}000 - 2{,}317{,}900 = 2{,}100$. This gives strong evidence to support choice D.

101. A carpenter with 400 one-by-four planks of wood wants to make at least 15 tables and 60 chairs. Each table requires 12 planks of wood and each chair requires 3 planks of wood. Which of the following systems of inequalities represents this situation, where t is the number of tables and c is the number of chairs the carpenter can make with the wood planks that he has?

A) $15t + 60c \leq 400$
$t \geq 15$
$c \geq 60$

B) $15t + 60c \leq 400$
$t \geq 12$
$c \geq 3$

C) $12t + 3c \leq 400$
$t \geq 15$
$c \geq 60$

D) $12t + 3c \leq 400$
$t \geq 12$
$c \geq 3$

(Setting Up Linear Systems)

* Since the carpenter wants to make at least 15 tables, we need $t \geq 15$. Similarly, since the carpenter wants to make at least 60 chairs, we need $c \geq 60$. This narrows the answer down to choices A and C.

Now, $12t$ is the number of planks of wood needed for the tables, and $3c$ is the number of planks of wood needed for the chairs. So, the total number of planks of wood needed is $12t + 3c$. We are told that the carpenter has 400 planks of wood, and so we must have $12t + 3c \leq 400$. So, the answer is choice **C**.

102. Lines k and m have equations $y = 5x + b$ and $y = ax - 5$, respectively. Given that the two lines intersect at the point $(-2, 7)$, what is the value of $b - a$?

(Equations of Lines and Their Graphs)

* The point $(-2, 7)$ lies on each line. For the first line, we have $7 = 5(-2) + b$, so that $7 = -10 + b$, and therefore, $b = 17$. For the second line, we have $7 = a(-2) - 5$, so that $7 = -2a - 5$, and therefore, $-2a = 12$. So, $a = \frac{12}{-2} = -6$. Finally, $b - a = 17 - (-6) = 17 + 6 = \mathbf{23}$.

103. Dr. Steve creates and sells SAT math problems. He sells "Heart of Algebra" problems for $15 per problem and he sells "Passport to Advanced Math" problems for $20 per problem. If an app developer purchased 97 problems from Dr. Steve for a total of $1780, how many "Heart of Algebra" problems did the developer purchase?

(Solving Linear Systems of Equations)

* Solution using the elimination method: Let's let h be the number of "Heart of Algebra" problems purchased, and p the number of "Passport to Advanced Math" problems purchased. Then we are given the following system of equations.

$$h + p = 97$$
$$15h + 20p = 1780$$

We will now multiply each side of the first equation by -20.

$$-20(h + p) = -20(97)$$
$$15h + 20p = 1780$$

Do not forget to distribute correctly on the left. Add the two equations.

$$\begin{array}{rcl} -20h - 20p &=& -1940 \\ 15h + 20p &=& \underline{1780} \\ -5h &=& -\ 160 \end{array}$$

We divide each side of this last equation by -5 to get

$$h = \frac{-160}{-5} = \mathbf{32}.$$

$$5x - 2y = c$$
$$-3x + 1.2y = -9$$

104. In the system of equations above, c is a constant and x and y are variables. If the system has infinitely many solutions (x, y), what is the value of c ?

(Advanced Linear Systems)

* We must have $\frac{5}{-3} = \frac{-2}{1.2} = \frac{c}{-9}$. In particular, we need $\frac{5}{-3} = \frac{c}{-9}$. Cross multiplying gives us $-3c = -45$. We divide by -3 to get $c = \frac{-45}{-3} = \mathbf{15}$.

Note: See Problem 72 for more information on this type of problem.

LEVEL 4: PASSPORT TO ADVANCED MATH

$$f(x) = x^2 - 3x + 2$$
$$g(x) = x^3 - 5x^2 + 6x$$

105. Which of the following expressions is equivalent to $\frac{f(x)}{g(x)}$, for $x \neq 0, 2,$ and 3 ?

A) $\frac{x-1}{x-3}$

B) $\frac{x-1}{x-2}$

C) $\frac{x-1}{x^2-3x}$

D) $\frac{x-1}{x^2-2x}$

(Factoring)

* $f(x) = x^2 - 3x + 2 = (x-2)(x-1)$

$g(x) = x^3 - 5x^2 + 6x = x(x^2 - 5x + 6) = x(x-2)(x-3)$

$$\frac{f(x)}{g(x)} = \frac{(x-2)(x-1)}{x(x-2)(x-3)} = \frac{x-1}{x(x-3)} = \frac{x-1}{x^2-3x}$$

This is choice **C**.

106. Which of the following is an example of a function whose graph in the xy-plane can have more than one x-intercept?

   I. A linear function whose rate of change is zero
   II. A quadratic function with no real zeros
   III. A cubic polynomial with at least one real zero

   A) I and II only
   B) I and III only
   C) III only
   D) I, II, and III

(Graphs of Functions)

* The line $y = 0$ (the x-axis) is a line whose rate of change is zero, and there are infinitely many x-intercepts. So, I works, and we can eliminate choice C.

If a function has no real zeros, then its graph does not have any x-intercepts. So, II does not work, and we can eliminate choices A and D.

Therefore, the answer is choice **B**.

Notes: (1) The expression "rate of change" is just another way of saying slope. So, a linear function with a rate of change of zero has a graph that is a horizontal line.

(2) Recall that a **polynomial** has the form $a_n x^n + a_{n-1} x^{n-1} + \cdots + a_1 x + a_0$ where $a_0, a_1, \ldots, a_n$ are real numbers. For example, $x^2 + 2x - 35$ is a polynomial. The **degree** of the polynomial is n. In other words, it is the highest power that appears in the expanded form of the polynomial.

A linear function (or linear polynomial) is a polynomial of degree 1.

A quadratic function (or quadratic polynomial) is a polynomial of degree 2.

A cubic function (or cubic polynomial) is a polynomial of degree 3.

(3) A polynomial of degree n has at most n x-intercepts.

In particular, a cubic polynomial has at most 3 x-intercepts.

(4) Recall that c is a **zero** of a polynomial $p(x)$ if $p(c) = 0$. If c is a real number, then this is equivalent to the point $(c, 0)$ being on the graph of p, or c being an x-intercept of the graph of p.

So, saying that a polynomial has no real zeros is the same thing as saying that the graph of p has no x-intercepts, and saying that a polynomial has at least one real zero is the same thing as saying that the graph of p has at least one x-intercept.

107. The expression $\dfrac{a^{\frac{1}{3}} b^{-5}}{a^{-4} b^{\frac{3}{2}}}$, where $a > 5$ and $b > 5$, is equivalent to which of the following?

A) $\dfrac{\sqrt[3]{a}}{\sqrt{b}}$

B) $\dfrac{a^2 \sqrt[3]{a}}{b^3 \sqrt{b}}$

C) $\dfrac{a^4 \sqrt[3]{a}}{b^6 \sqrt{b}}$

D) $\dfrac{a^5}{b^7}$

(Exponents and Roots)

* Solution using laws of exponents:

$$\frac{a^{\frac{1}{3}} b^{-5}}{a^{-4} b^{\frac{3}{2}}} = a^{\frac{1}{3} - (-4)} b^{-5 - \frac{3}{2}} = a^{\frac{1}{3} + 4} b^{-5 - \frac{3}{2}} = a^{\frac{1}{3} + \frac{12}{3}} b^{-\frac{10}{2} - \frac{3}{2}} = a^{\frac{13}{3}} b^{-\frac{13}{2}} = \frac{a^{\frac{13}{3}}}{b^{\frac{13}{2}}} = \frac{\sqrt[3]{a^{13}}}{\sqrt{b^{13}}} = \frac{\sqrt[3]{a^{12} a^1}}{\sqrt{b^{12} b^1}} = \frac{a^4 \sqrt[3]{a}}{b^6 \sqrt{b}}$$

This is choice **C**.

Notes: (1) For the first step, we used the law of exponents in the fourth row of the table (after Problem 10) two times.

(2) For the second step, we wrote $\frac{1}{3} - (-4) = \frac{1}{3} + 4$.

(3) For the third step, we found that the least common denominator between $\frac{1}{3}$ and 4 is 3, and we wrote $4 = \frac{4}{1} \cdot \frac{3}{3} = \frac{12}{3}$. We also found that the least common denominator between -5 and $-\frac{3}{2}$ is 2, and we wrote $-5 = \frac{-5}{1} \cdot \frac{2}{2} = -\frac{10}{2}$.

(4) For the fourth step, we added $\frac{1}{3} + \frac{12}{3} = \frac{1+12}{3} = \frac{13}{3}$ and $-\frac{10}{2} - \frac{3}{2} = \frac{-10-3}{2} = -\frac{13}{2}$.

(5) For the fifth step, we used the law of exponents in the fourth row of the table (after Problem 10) again.

(6) For the sixth step, we used the law of exponents in the eleventh row of the table (after Problem 10) twice.

(7) For the seventh step, we factored a^{13} as $a^{12}a^1$. Notice that 12 is divisible by 3, so that a^{12} is a perfect cube. Similarly, we factored b^{13} as $b^{12}b^1$. In this case, it is important that 12 is even, so that b^{12} is a perfect square.

(8) For the last step, we used the laws of exponents in the fifth, sixth, tenth, and eleventh rows of the table (after Problem 10), to get

$$\sqrt[3]{a^{12}a^1} = (a^{12}a^1)^{\frac{1}{3}} = (a^{12})^{\frac{1}{3}}(a^1)^{\frac{1}{3}} = a^{\frac{12}{3}} \cdot a^{\frac{1}{3}} = a^4\sqrt[3]{a}$$

and

$$\sqrt{b^{12}b^1} = (b^{12}b^1)^{\frac{1}{2}} = (b^{12})^{\frac{1}{2}}(b^1)^{\frac{1}{2}} = b^{\frac{12}{2}} \cdot b^{\frac{1}{2}} = b^6\sqrt{b}$$

(9) This problem can also be solved by picking numbers. I leave the details to the reader.

$$x^2 + 5x + \frac{1}{4}$$

108. Which of the following expressions is equivalent to the expression above?

A) $\left(x - \frac{5}{2}\right)^2 + 6$

B) $\left(x - \frac{5}{2}\right)^2 - 6$

C) $\left(x + \frac{5}{2}\right)^2 + 6$

D) $\left(x + \frac{5}{2}\right)^2 - 6$

(Manipulating Nonlinear Expressions)

* **Solution by completing the square:** Half of 5 is $\frac{5}{2}$, and when we square $\frac{5}{2}$, we get $\frac{25}{4}$. So, we add and subtract $\frac{25}{4}$ to the expression to get $x^2 + 5x + \frac{25}{4} - \frac{25}{4} + \frac{1}{4} = \left(x + \frac{5}{2}\right)^2 - \frac{24}{4} = \left(x + \frac{5}{2}\right)^2 - 6$, choice **D**.

Notes: (1) To complete the square on the expression $x^2 + bx$, we take half of the number b, and square the result to get b^2.

For example, to complete the square on $x^2 + 5x$, we take half of 5 to get $\frac{5}{2}$, and then square $\frac{5}{2}$ to get $\left(\frac{5}{2}\right)^2 = \frac{5^2}{2^2} = \frac{25}{4}$.

We then add this to the original expression to get $x^2 + 5x + \frac{25}{4}$. This new expression is a perfect square. In fact, it factors as follows:

$$x^2 + 5x + \frac{25}{4} = \left(x + \frac{5}{2}\right)\left(x + \frac{5}{2}\right) = \left(x + \frac{5}{2}\right)^2$$

Note that the number $\frac{5}{2}$ is the same as the number we got from taking half of 5. This is not a coincidence. It always happens.

(2) Completing the square *does not* produce an expression that is equivalent to the original expression. For example, the expression $\left(x + \frac{5}{2}\right)^2 = x^2 + 5x + \frac{25}{4}$ is $\frac{25}{4}$ more than the original expression $x^2 + 5x$.

We can fix this problem by subtracting what we just added. We have

$$x^2 + 5x = x^2 + 5x + \frac{25}{4} - \frac{25}{4} = \left(x + \frac{5}{2}\right)^2 - \frac{25}{4}$$

(3) Finally, we have

$$x^2 + 5x + \frac{1}{4} = \left(x + \frac{5}{2}\right)^2 - \frac{25}{4} + \frac{1}{4} = \left(x + \frac{5}{2}\right)^2 - \frac{24}{2} = \left(x + \frac{5}{2}\right)^2 - 6.$$

109. Which of the following equations has a graph in the xy-plane with two x-intercepts?

       A) $y = x^2 + 4$
       B) $y = -x^2 - 1$
       C) $y = 3(x - 1)^2$
       D) $y = x^2 - x - 2$

(Graphs of Parabolas)

Solution by process of elimination using basic transformations: The graph of $y = x^2$ is an upward facing parabola with vertex at the origin. We shift this graph up 4 units to get the graph of $y = x^2 + 4$. So, the graph of $y = x^2 + 4$ has no x-intercepts, and we can eliminate choice A.

We reflect the graph of $y = x^2$ in the x-axis to get the graph of $y = -x^2$. So, this latter graph is a downward facing parabola with vertex at the origin. We shift this last graph down 1 unit to get the graph of $y = -x^2 - 1$. It follows that the graph of $y = -x^2 - 1$ has no x-intercepts, and we can eliminate choice B.

We move the graph of $y = x^2$ right 1 unit to get the graph of $y = (x - 1)^2$. The latter graph is therefore an upward facing parabola with vertex $(1, 0)$. Multiplying by 3 causes a vertical expansion that does not affect the position of its vertex. So, the graph of $y = 3(x - 1)^2$ has one x-intercept, and we can eliminate choice C.

By process of elimination, the answer is choice **D**.

Notes: (1) If a calculator is allowed for the question, we can put each equation in our graphing calculator and graph each in a standard window to see the x-intercepts. The reasoning used in this solution, however, can get you the answer much faster.

(2) We can verify that the graph of $y = x^2 - x - 2$ has two x-intercepts in several different ways. Here are a few different methods.

Method 1: The discriminant of the equation $y = ax^2 + bx + c$ is $b^2 - 4ac$. Here we have $a = 1$, $b = -1$, and $c = -2$. The discriminant is $b^2 - 4ac = (-1)^2 - 4 \cdot 1(-2) = 1 + 8 = 9$. Since the discriminant is positive, there are two x-intercepts. (If the discriminant were 0, there would be one x-intercept, and if the discriminant were negative, there would be no x-intercepts.)

Method 2: We can factor the right-hand side to get $y = (x - 2)(x + 1)$. We can now clearly see that there are two x-intercepts: $x = 2$ and $x = -1$.

Method 3: We can find the x-coordinate of the vertex. Using the formula $x = -\frac{b}{2a}$. Here, we get $x = -\frac{-1}{2 \cdot 1} = \frac{1}{2}$. We then substitute this into the equation to get the y-coordinate of the vertex. Here, we get $y = \left(\frac{1}{2}\right)^2 - \frac{1}{2} - 2 = \frac{1}{4} - \frac{2}{4} - \frac{8}{4} = -\frac{9}{4}$. Since the y-coordinate of the vertex is negative and the parabola opens upward (because $a = 1 > 0$), the graph must hit the x-axis twice.

(3) Let $y = f(x)$, and $k > 0$. We can move the graph of f around by applying the following basic transformations.

$y = f(x) + k$	shift up k units
$y = f(x) - k$	shift down k units
$y = f(x - k)$	shift right k units
$y = f(x + k)$	shift left k units
$y = -f(x)$	reflect in x-axis
$y = f(-x)$	reflect in y-axis.

Solution by process of elimination and finding the vertices: Choices A, B, and C are in standard form and so we can pick out the vertices on their graphs just by looking at the equations.

The graph of $y = x^2 + 4$ has vertex $(0, 4)$ and it opens upwards, so there are no x-intercepts and we can eliminate choice A.

The graph of $y = -x^2 - 1$ has vertex $(0, -1)$ and it opens downward, so there are no x-intercepts and we can eliminate choice B.

The graph of $y = 3(x - 1)^2$ has vertex $(1, 0)$. Since the vertex lies on the x-axis, the vertex is the only x-intercept and we can eliminate choice C.

Therefore, by process of elimination, the answer is choice **D**.

Note: The **standard form for a quadratic function** is

$$y - k = a(x - h)^2 \quad \text{or} \quad y = a(x - h)^2 + k$$

The graph is a parabola with **vertex** at (h, k). The parabola opens upwards if $a > 0$ and downwards if $a < 0$.

110. If $x^4 - y^4 = a$, $x^2 - y^2 = b$, and $x^2 + y^2 = c$, where b and c are nonzero constants, what is the value of $\frac{a}{bc}$?

(Factoring)

* **Solution using the difference of two squares:**
$a = x^4 - y^4 = (x^2 - y^2)(x^2 + y^2) = bc$. So, $\frac{a}{bc} = \frac{a}{a} = \mathbf{1}$.

111. If $x > 0$ and $x = \sqrt[3]{\frac{16x}{9}}$, what is the value of x ?

(Exponents and Roots)

* We cube each side of the equation to get $x^3 = \frac{16x}{9}$. We now multiply by 9 to get $9x^3 = 16x$. We subtract $16x$ from each side of this last equation and get $9x^3 - 16x = 0$. Factoring on the left gives us $x(9x^2 - 16) = x(3x - 4)(3x + 4)$. So, $x = 0$, $3x - 4 = 0$, or $3x + 4 = 0$. Solving the last two equations for x gives us $x = \frac{4}{3}$ or $x = -\frac{4}{3}$. It follows that the three solutions to the equation are 0, $\frac{4}{3}$, and $-\frac{4}{3}$. Since we are looking for the positive solution, the answer is **4/3** or **1.33**.

112. If $x > 0$ and $3x^2 - 2x - 5 = 0$, what is the value of x ?

(Solving Quadratic Equations)

* **Solution by factoring:** $3x^2 - 2x - 5 = (x + 1)(3x - 5)$. So, we have $x + 1 = 0$ or $3x - 5 = 0$. Therefore, $x = -1$ or $x = \frac{5}{3}$. Since we want the positive solution, we grid in **5/3**, **1.66**, or **1.67**.

Note: We can solve the quadratic equation $3x^2 - 2x - 5 = 0$ in several other ways. Here is is one more method:

Quadratic formula: We identify $a = 3$, $b = -2$, and $c = -5$.

$$x = \frac{-b \pm \sqrt{b^2 - 4ac}}{2a} = \frac{2 \pm \sqrt{4 + 60}}{2 \cdot 3} = \frac{2 \pm \sqrt{64}}{6} = \frac{2 \pm 8}{6}.$$

So, we get $x = \frac{2+8}{6} = \frac{10}{6} = \frac{5}{3}$ or $x = \frac{2-8}{6} = -\frac{6}{6} = -1$. Since we are given $x > 0$, $x = \frac{5}{3}$.

LEVEL 4: PROBLEM SOLVING

Questions 113 - 114 refer to the following information.

$$r = \sqrt{\frac{P}{4\pi I}}$$

Given that the power of the radio signal from a radio antenna is P, the distance from the radio antenna r is related to the intensity of the signal I by the formula above.

113. Which of the following expresses the power of the radio signal in terms of the distance from the radio antenna and the intensity of the signal?

    A) $P = 4\pi I r^2$

    B) $P = \frac{4\pi I}{r^2}$

    C) $P = \frac{r^2}{4\pi I}$

    D) $P = \frac{I}{4\pi r^2}$

(Ratios)

* Algebraic solution: We square each side of the given equation to get $r^2 = \frac{P}{4\pi I}$. We then multiply each side of this last equation by $4\pi I$ to get $4\pi I r^2 = P$. So, the answer is choice **A**.

Solution by picking numbers: Let's let $P = \pi$ and $I = 1$. It follows that

$$r = \sqrt{\frac{\pi}{4\pi}} = \sqrt{\frac{1}{4}} = \frac{\sqrt{1}}{\sqrt{4}} = \frac{1}{2}.$$

Substituting $P = \pi$, $r = \frac{1}{2}$ and $I = 1$ into each answer choice yields false equations for choices B, C, and D (check this!). So, the answer must be choice **A**.

Note: When picking numbers, remember to check all four answer choices!

114. Emily and Amanda are measuring the intensity of a radio signal coming from the same antenna. Amanda is five times as far from the antenna as Emily. Amanda's measurement is what fraction of Emily's measurement?

    A) $\frac{1}{5}$

    B) $\frac{1}{25}$

    C) $\frac{1}{150}$

    D) $\frac{1}{625}$

(Ratios)

85

Solution by picking numbers: Let's let the power be $P = 1$. Then we have $I = \frac{P}{4\pi r^2} = \frac{1}{4\pi r^2}$ (check this). Let's let Emily's distance be 1 and Amanda's distance be 5. Then for Emily, the intensity is $I = \frac{1}{4\pi \cdot 1^2} = \frac{1}{4\pi}$, and for Amanda, the intensity is $I = \frac{1}{4\pi \cdot 5^2} = \frac{1}{100\pi}$.

Finally, we have $\frac{1}{100\pi} \div \frac{1}{4\pi} = \frac{1}{100\pi} \cdot \frac{4\pi}{1} = \frac{1}{25}$, choice **B**.

* **Direct solution:** If Emily's distance is r, then Amanda's distance is $5r$, and we have $\frac{P}{4\pi(5r)^2} \div \frac{P}{4\pi r^2} = \frac{P}{4\pi \cdot 25r^2} \cdot \frac{4\pi r^2}{P} = \frac{1}{25}$, choice **B**.

Questions 116 - 118 refer to the following information.

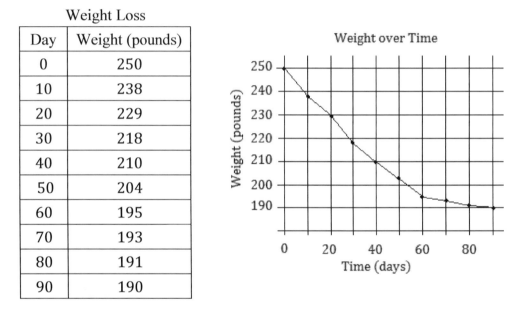

Weight Loss

Day	Weight (pounds)
0	250
10	238
20	229
30	218
40	210
50	204
60	195
70	193
80	191
90	190

A study was conducted on how a certain nutritional supplement affects weight loss. The table and graph above show the weight w, in pounds, of a single male subject t days after he began taking the supplement.

115. The function w, defined by $w(t) = -mt + b$, where m and b are constants, models the weight, in pounds, of the subject t days after he began taking the supplement during a span of time in which the weight loss of the subject is approximately linear. What does m represent?

    A) The predicated weight, in pounds, of the subject at the beginning of the time span
    B) The predicted weight, in pounds, of the subject at the end of the time span
    C) The predicted amount of weight the subject loses each day
    D) The predicted total increase in weight of the subject, in pounds, during the time span

(Graphs)

* m is the slope of the line segment. So, we have

$$m = \text{Slope} = \frac{\text{change in the dependent variable}}{\text{change in the independent variable}} = \frac{\text{change in } w}{\text{change in } t}$$

So, m is the predicted change in the weight of the subject per day. Since there is a minus sign in front of the m, the word "change" can be replaced with "decrease." So, m represents the predicted amount of weight the subject loses each day, choice **C**.

116. * The rate at which the subject's weight is changing from day 10 through day 40 is nearly constant. On this interval, which of the following equations best models the weight w, in pounds, of the subject t days after the subject began using the supplement?

   A) $w(t) = -0.93t + 247$
   B) $w(t) = -t + 260$
   C) $w(t) = -1.3t + 270$
   D) $w(t) = -2.01t + 247$

(Graphs)

* We can estimate the slope of the line using the points $(10, 238)$ and $(40, 210)$. Using these points, we get $m \approx \frac{210 - 238}{40 - 10} = \frac{-28}{30} \approx -0.93$. So, the answer must be choice **A**.

Notes: (1) Since choice A has the only equation with a slope of -0.93, we do not need to finish writing the equation of the line.

(2) For completeness, let's approximate an equation of the line passing through the points $(10, 238)$ and $(40, 210)$. We already found that the slope is approximately -0.93. Let's use the point $(10, 238)$ and write an equation of the line in point-slope form. We get $y - 238 = -0.93(t - 10)$. Distributing on the right-hand side, we get $y - 238 = -0.93x + 9.3$. We now add 238 to each side of the equation to get $y = -0.93x + 247.3$. This is very close to the equation given in choice A.

117. Over which of the following time periods is the average decay rate of the subject's weight least?

   A) Day 0 to Day 20
   B) Day 20 to Day 40
   C) Day 40 to Day 60
   D) Day 60 to Day 90

(Graphs)

* The function is decreasing the least from Day 60 to Day 90, choice **D**.

Note: We can compute the average decay rates by finding the absolute values of the slopes of the appropriate line segments. In other words, we find the slope of each line segment, and then just "forget" about the minus sign. Let's do this for each answer choice.

A) $m = \frac{229-250}{20-0} = -1.05$ Average decay rate = 1.05

B) $m = \frac{210-229}{40-20} = -0.95$ Average decay rate = 0.95

C) $m = \frac{195-210}{60-40} = -0.75$ Average decay Rate = 0.75

D) $m = \frac{190-195}{90-60} \approx -0.167$ Average decay rate $\approx$ 0.167

118. A research study was conducted to determine if a certain supplement is successful in promoting weight loss in women weighing more than 180 pounds. From a large population of women weighing more than 180 pounds, 500 participants were randomly selected. Half of the women were given the supplement, and the other half were given a placebo. The resulting data showed that women who received the actual supplement had lost significantly more weight than those who received the placebo. Based on the design and results of the study, which of the following is the most appropriate conclusion?

A) The supplement will cause significant weight loss.
B) The supplement will cause weight loss in all women who take it.
C) The supplement is likely to cause weight loss in women who weigh more than 180 pounds.
D) The supplement is better than any other weight loss regimen for women weighing more than 180 pounds.

(Data Analysis)

* The population mentioned in this problem consists of women weighing more than 180 pounds. We can therefore generalize the results to this population only and the answer is choice **C**.

Notes: (1) **Don't change the population.** The results from one population DO NOT carry over to another population.

Choice B mentions "all women." This is a different population than "women weighing more than 180 pounds." Since results from one population do not carry over to another population, we can eliminate choice B.

(2) Choice A has two problems. The first is that no population is mentioned and so we are to assume that the result holds in general. However, as mentioned in Note (1), results from one population do not carry over to another population. The other problem with choice A is that it is too extreme. We might be able to say that the supplement is likely to cause weight loss (as long as we stay inside the appropriate population, of course), but we can never say that it will cause weight loss with absolute certainty every time. We can eliminate choice A for either of these two reasons.

(3) Choice D is comparing the supplement to other weight loss regimens. But no other weight loss regimens were used in the study. Therefore, we cannot say anything about the relationship between this supplement and other weight loss regimens, and so, we can eliminate choice D.

119. The first family of deer arrived on Staten Island in 2007, and since then the deer population has been doubling every six months. Which of the following statements describes the type of function that best models the relationship between the number of six-month time periods and the population of deer on Staten Island?

   A) Linear growth because the population of deer is increasing by the same amount every six months
   B) Linear growth because the population of deer is increasing by the same percentage every six months
   C) Exponential growth because the population of deer is increasing by the same amount every six months
   D) Exponential growth because the population of deer is increasing by the same percentage every six months

(Growth)

* "Doubling" is another way of saying "increasing at a growth rate of 100%" (see Example 1 in Note 2 below). So, the deer population is increasing by the same percentage every six months. We can therefore eliminate choices A and C.

Now, relationships that increase by the same percentage every time period are exponential, and so the answer is choice **D**.

Notes: (1) A relationship is linear if it changes by a constant amount and a relationship is exponential if it changes by a constant percentage.

(2) A general **exponential function** has the form $f(t) = a(1 + r)^{ct}$, where $a = f(0)$ is the *initial amount* and r is the *growth rate*. If $r > 0$, then we have **exponential growth** and if $r < 0$, we have **exponential decay**.

Example 1: The exponential function $f(t) = 300(2)^t$ can be used to model a population with a growth rate of $1 = 100\%$ each year that begins with 300 specimens. The growth rate of 100% tells us that the population doubles each year.

Example 2: The exponential function $f(t) = 50(3)^{2t}$ can be used to model a population with a growth rate of $2 = 200\%$ every 6 months that begins with 50 specimens. The growth rate of 200% tells us that the population triples. Since $c = 2$, the tripling occurs every $\frac{1}{2}$ year or 6 months.

Example 3: The exponential function $f(t) = 120(0.75)^{\frac{t}{3}}$ can be used to model a substance which is decaying at a rate of $1 - 0.75 = 0.25 = 25\%$ every 3 years. The initial amount of the substance might be 120 grams. Since $c = \frac{1}{3}$, the 25% decay occurs every 3 years.

Example 4: A quantity that continually doubles over a fixed time period can be modeled by the exponential function $f(t) = a(2)^{\frac{t}{d}}$ where a is the quantity at time $t = 0$, and d is the doubling time in years.

120. An educational workshop is attended by students, teachers, tutors, administrators, and parents. Of those attending, 10% are students, 15% are teachers, 12% are tutors, 23% are administrators, and the remaining 80 people are parents. Assuming that each person in attendance has exactly one of the five roles (for example, no teacher is also an administrator), how many more teachers are in attendance than tutors?

(Percents)

* If we let x represent the total number of people attending the workshop, then we have $0.10x + 0.15x + 0.12x + 0.23x + 80 = x$. Combining like terms on the left gives $0.60x + 80 = x$. We subtract $0.60x$ from each side of this equation to get $80 = x - 0.60x = (1 - 0.60)x = 0.40x$. Dividing each side of this last equation by 0.40 gives us $x = \frac{80}{0.40} = 200$. The number of teachers in attendance is $0.15x = 0.15 \cdot 200 = 30$ and the number of tutors in attendance is $0.12 \cdot 200 = 24$. So, the answer is $30 - 24 = \mathbf{6}$.

LEVEL 4: GEOMETRY AND COMPLEX NUMBERS

121. The surface area A of a sphere can be expressed in terms of the volume V of the sphere and the diameter d of the sphere by the formula $A = \frac{6V}{d}$. Which of the following expresses the circumference C of the sphere in terms of its surface area and radius?

A) $C = \frac{4\pi^2 r^3}{A}$

B) $C = \frac{8\pi^2 r^3}{A}$

C) $C = \frac{4A}{\pi^2 r^3}$

D) $C = \frac{8A}{\pi^2 r^3}$

(Solid Geometry)

* The volume of a sphere is given by the formula $V = \frac{4}{3}\pi r^3$, and the diameter of the sphere is given by $d = 2r$, where r is the radius of the sphere. Therefore, we have $A = \frac{6\left(\frac{4}{3}\pi r^3\right)}{2r}$, or equivalently, $2rA = 8\pi r^3$. We multiply each side of the equation by π to get $2\pi rA = 8\pi^2 r^3$, or equivalently, $CA = 8\pi^2 r^3$. Finally, we divide each side of this equation by A to get $C = \frac{8\pi^2 r^3}{A}$, choice **B**.

Notes: (1) The formula for the circumference of a sphere is the same formula as for the circumference of a circle: $C = 2\pi r$. Therefore, we need to make sure that $2\pi r$ appears in the expression. This is why we multiply each side of the equation $2rA = 8\pi r^3$ by π.

(2) The circumference formula can also be written as $C = \pi d$. So, we do not really need to replace d by $2r$. We can instead multiply each side of the given equation by d to get $dA = 6V = 6 \cdot \frac{4}{3}\pi r^3$, and then multiply each side of this last equation by π to get $CA = \pi dA = 8\pi^2 r^3$.

(3) This problem can also be solved by picking numbers. Try choosing a value for r, computing d, V, A, and C, and then substituting the values for r and A into each answer choice. I leave the details to the reader.

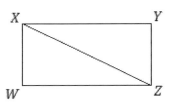

122. In the figure above, $XYZW$ is a rectangle. Which of the following must be true?

    A) $\cos \angle WXZ = \sin \angle YXZ$
    B) $\cos \angle WXZ = \sin \angle XZY$
    C) $\cos \angle WZX = \sin \angle YXZ$
    D) $\cos \angle ZXY = \sin \angle XZW$

(Trigonometry)

* Solution using a cofunction identity: Angles WXZ and YXZ have measures that sum to $90°$. It follows that $\cos \angle WXZ = \sin \angle YXZ$, choice **A**.

Notes: (1) Since $XYZW$ is a rectangle, we have $m\angle WXY = 90°$. So, $m\angle WXZ + m\angle YXZ = 90°$.

(2) See Problem 94 for the cofunction identities and how to use them. For this problem, all we need to know is that the cofunction identities say that if the measures of two angles sum to $90°$, then the cosine of one of the angles is equal to the sine of the other angle.

(3) Since $XYZW$ is a rectangle, $\overline{XY}$ and $\overline{WZ}$ are parallel. It follows that angles WXZ and XZY have the same measure (alternate interior angles). Since $\cos x = \sin x$ is not *always* true, we can eliminate choice B. A similar argument allows us to eliminate choices C and D as well.

123. The height of a trapezoid is doubled and each base of the trapezoid is reduced by 25%. How does the area of the trapezoid change?

    A) The area of the trapezoid does not change.
    B) The area of the trapezoid is doubled.
    C) The area of the trapezoid is increased by 50%.
    D) The area of the trapezoid is reduced by 50%

(Polygons)

* Algebraic solution: Let b_1, b_2, h, and A be the two bases, the height, and the area of the original trapezoid, respectively, so that we have $A = \frac{1}{2}(b_1 + b_2) \cdot h$. Let A' be the new area after the bases and height are changed. We have

$$A' = \frac{1}{2}\left(\frac{3}{4}b_1 + \frac{3}{4}b_2\right) \cdot 2h = 2 \cdot \frac{3}{4} \cdot \frac{1}{2}(b_1 + b_2) \cdot h = \frac{3}{2} \cdot \frac{1}{2}(b_1 + b_2) \cdot h = \frac{3}{2}A = 1.5A$$

So, the area would be increased by 50%, choice **C**.

Notes: (1) To get the area of a trapezoid we average the two bases and then multiply by the height. Formally, $A = \frac{1}{2}(b_1 + b_2) \cdot h$.

(2) Reducing a number by 25% is the same as taking $(100 - 25)\% = 75\%$ of the number. This is the same as multiplying the number by $\frac{75}{100} = \frac{3}{4}$.

This is why we replace b_1 and b_2 by $\frac{3}{4}b_1$ and $\frac{3}{4}b_2$, respectively.

(3) To double the height means to multiply the height by 2.

(4) Using the distributive property, we have $\frac{3}{4}b_1 + \frac{3}{4}b_2 = \frac{3}{4}(b_1 + b_2)$.

Solution by picking numbers: Let's let $b_1 = 10$, $b_2 = 12$, and $h = 2$ so that $A = \frac{1}{2}(10 + 12) \cdot 2 = 22$ is the area of the original trapezoid. The area of the new trapezoid is then $A' = \frac{1}{2}(7.5 + 9) \cdot 4 = 33$. Since $33 = 1.5 \cdot 22 = 150\%$ of $22 = 50\%$ more than 22, the answer is choice **C**.

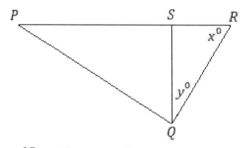

Note: Figure not drawn to scale.

124. In the figure above, if $x = 35$, $PQ \perp QR$, and $PQ = PS$, what is the value of y ?

(Lines and Angles and Triangles)

* We are given that $\overline{PQ}$ is perpendicular to $\overline{QR}$. It follows that the measure of angle PQR is 90°. Since $x = 35$, the measure of angle QPR is $180 - 90 - 35 = 55°$. Now, since $PQ = PS$, the angles opposite these sides are congruent. Thus, angle PQS has measure $\frac{180-55}{2} = 62.5$. So, we have $y = 90 - 62.5 = \mathbf{27.5}$.

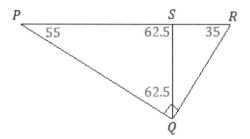

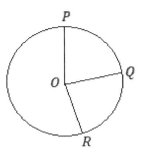

125. In the circle above, radius $\overline{OP}$ has length 2, the length of arc $\widehat{PQ}$ is $\frac{7\pi}{9}$, and $m\angle POQ = m\angle QOR$. What is the measure, in degrees, or $\angle POR$? (Disregard the degree symbol when gridding your answer.)

(Circles)

* **Solution by setting up a ratio:** The circumference of the circle is $C = 2\pi r = 2\pi \cdot 2 = 4\pi$. The length of arc $\widehat{PR}$ is $2 \cdot \frac{7\pi}{9} = \frac{14\pi}{9}$. We can now find the measure of $\angle POR$ by setting up a ratio

arc	$\frac{14\pi}{9}$	4π
degrees	x	360

$$\frac{\frac{14\pi}{9}}{x} = \frac{4\pi}{360} \Rightarrow 4\pi x = \frac{14\pi}{9} \cdot 360 = 560\pi \Rightarrow x = \frac{560\pi}{4\pi} = \textbf{140}$$

Solution using a formula: We can also use the formula $s = r\theta$ to find $\theta = m\angle POQ$ in radians. In this formula, r is the radius, θ is an angle in radians, and s is the length of the arc that the angle intercepts. So, for this problem, we have $s = \frac{7\pi}{9}$ and $r = 2$. So, using $s = r\theta$, we have $\frac{7\pi}{9} = 2\theta$, and therefore, $\theta = \frac{7\pi}{18}$.

Now, $m\angle POR = 2m\angle POQ = 2 \cdot \frac{7\pi}{18} = \frac{7\pi}{9}$. Finally, we change the angle from radians to degrees by replacing π by 180. We get $\frac{7 \cdot 180}{9} = \textbf{140}$ (see the quickest solution from Problem 61).

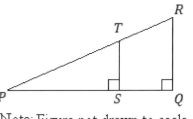

Note: Figure not drawn to scale.

126. In the figure above, $\overline{ST} \parallel \overline{QR}$ and $\overline{QS}$ is one-third the length of $\overline{PS}$. The area of ΔPQR is 16 and the lengths of $\overline{ST}$ and $\overline{QR}$ are integers. What is one possible length of $\overline{ST}$?

(Parallel Lines and Similarity)

* Let's let $PS = x$ and $QR = y$. Then $QS = \frac{1}{3}x$ and $PQ = x + \frac{1}{3}x = \frac{4}{3}x$.

Using the formula for the area of a triangle, $A = \frac{1}{2}bh$, we have $16 = \frac{1}{2} \cdot \frac{4}{3}xy = \frac{2}{3}xy$, and so $xy = 24$.

Let's try $x = 3$ and $y = 8$. Then $PS = 3$, $QS = \frac{1}{3} \cdot 3 = 1$, and $PQ = PS + QS = 3 + 1 = 4$.

Since $\Delta PST \sim \Delta PQR$, we have $\frac{QR}{PQ} = \frac{ST}{PS}$. So, $\frac{8}{4} = \frac{ST}{3} \Rightarrow 4ST = 24 \Rightarrow ST = \frac{24}{4} = \mathbf{6}$.

Notes: (1) Using the given information, we found that xy needs to equal 24. We also know that $y = QR$ needs to be an integer. So, y can be 1, 2, 3, 4, 6, 8, 12, or 24. We chose to let $y = 8$ from which it follows that $x = 3$ and $ST = 6$.

Other choices for y will lead to different values for ST. Be careful because some choices for y will lead to noninteger values for ST.

(2) The acceptable answers to this question are 3, 6, 9, and 18. See if you can figure out which choices for x and y lead to these values for ST.

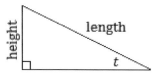

127. A contractor built a ramp such that the sine of angle t, as shown in the figure above, is $\frac{1}{6}$. If the ramp is 10 feet long, what is the height of the ramp, in feet?

(Trigonometry)

*

$$\frac{1}{6} = \sin t = \frac{\text{OPP}}{\text{HYP}} = \frac{\text{height}}{\text{length}} = \frac{\text{height}}{10}$$

So, height $= \frac{1}{6} \cdot 10 = \mathbf{5/3}$ or $\mathbf{1.66}$ or $\mathbf{1.67}$.

Note: See Problem 28 for a review of the trigonometry needed to solve this problem.

128. * If $i = \sqrt{-1}$, what is the quotient when $\frac{5-i^2}{i^2-7}$ is divided by $\frac{i^4-5}{8-i^4}$?

(Complex Numbers)

* $i^2 = -1$ and $i^4 = 1$. So, $\frac{5-i^2}{i^2-7} = \frac{5-(-1)}{-1-7} = \frac{5+1}{-8} = \frac{6}{-8}$ and $\frac{i^4-5}{8-i^4} = \frac{1-5}{8-1} = \frac{-4}{7}$. Therefore, we have $\frac{5-i^2}{i^2-7} \div \frac{i^4-5}{8-i^4} = \frac{6}{-8} \div \frac{-4}{7} = \frac{6}{-8} \cdot \frac{7}{-4} = \frac{42}{32} = 1.3125$

So, we grid in $\mathbf{1.31}$.

LEVEL 5: HEART OF ALGEBRA

129. The daily cost for a publishing company to produce x books is $C(x) = 4x + 800$. The company sells each book for \$36. Let $P(x) = R(x) - C(x)$, where $R(x)$ is the total income that the company gets for selling x books. The company takes a loss for the day if $P(x) < 0$. Which of the following inequalities gives all possible integer values of x that guarantee that the company will not take a loss on a given day?

    A) $x > 24$
    B) $x < 24$
    C) $x > 144$
    D) $x < 144$

(Solving Linear Inequalities)

* **Algebraic solution:** First note that $R(x) = 36x$, so that

$$P(x) = 36x - (4x + 800) = 36x - 4x - 800 = 32x - 800.$$

The company will not take a loss if $P(x) \geq 0$. So, we solve the inequality $32x - 800 \geq 0$ for x. Adding 800 to each side of this inequality yields $32x \geq 800$, so $x \geq \frac{800}{32} = 25$.

Since we are looking only at integer values for x, $x \geq 25$ is equivalent to $x > 24$, choice **A**.

Notes: (1) Income that a company receives is called **revenue**. A revenue function $R(x)$ gives the amount of income the company receives for selling x items.

If the company receives a fixed amount of d dollars per item, then the revenue function is $R(x) = dx$.

In this problem, the company receives 36 dollars per item, and so $R(x) = 36x$.

If the company sells 1 book, then the revenue is $R(1) = 36 \cdot 1 = 36$ dollars.

If the company sells 2 books, then the revenue is $R(2) = 36 \cdot 2 = 72$ dollars.

And so on...

(2) A company's **profit** is revenue minus cost. A profit function $P(x)$ gives the amount of profit (or loss) the company makes (or loses) if it sells x items.

$$P(x) = R(x) - C(x)$$

If revenue is greater than cost, then $P(x) > 0$, and the company makes a profit of $P(x)$ dollars.

If revenue is less than cost, then $P(x) < 0$, and the company takes a loss of $|P(x)|$ dollars.

The **break-even point** occurs when $P(x) = 0$.

In this problem, the break-even point occurs when 25 books are sold.

(3) When simplifying $P(x)$, make sure you are using the distributive property correctly. A common mistake would be to write

$$36x - (4x + 800) = 36x - 4x + 800.$$

This error comes from forgetting to distribute the minus sign.

If you frequently fall into this trap, it might help to first rewrite the expression $-(4x + 800)$ as $-1(4x + 800)$. So, we have

$$-(4x + 800) = -1(4x + 800) = -4x - 800.$$

(4) In general, $x \geq 25$ and $x > 24$ are not equivalent expressions. For example, if x is allowed to range over all real numbers, then $x = 24.5$ satisfies the second inequality, but not the first.

In this question however we are restricting our x-values to positive integers. In this case, the two inequalities are equivalent.

(5) $P(x) \geq 0$ is equivalent to $R(x) \geq C(x)$. So, we could also solve the inequality $36x \geq 4x + 800$. This method of solution avoids having to use the distributive property. We simply subtract $4x$ from each side of the inequality to get $32x \geq 800$, and then divide by 32 to get $x \geq 25$.

Solution by picking a number: Using the answer choices as a guide, let's choose a value for x, say $x = 50$.

Then $R(x) = R(50) = 36 \cdot 50 = 1800$, and $C(x) = C(50) = 4 \cdot 50 + 800 = 200 + 800 = 1000$.

So, $P(x) = R(x) - C(x) = 1800 - 1000 = 800$.

Thus, for $x = 50$, the company *does not* take a loss. Therefore, $x = 50$ should be a solution to the inequality. So, we can eliminate choices B and C.

We still need to decide if the answer is choice A or D. So, let's pick another number, say $x = 20$.

Then $R(x) = R(20) = 36 \cdot 20 = 720$, and $C(x) = C(20) = 4 \cdot 20 + 800 = 80 + 800 = 880$.

So, $P(x) = R(x) - C(x) = 720 - 880 = -160$.

Thus, for $x = 20$, the company *does* take a loss. Therefore, $x = 20$ should *not* be a solution to the inequality. So, we can eliminate choice D, and therefore the answer is choice **A**.

130. A music production company pays a songwriter a royalty of $0.20 per song downloaded for the first 300 downloads. After the first 300 downloads, the songwriter's royalty increases to $0.30 per song. Which of the following functions gives the songwriter's total royalty payment, $R(x)$, in dollars, in terms of the number of songs downloaded, where $x > 300$?

A) $R(x) = 0.20x + 0.30x$
B) $R(x) = 0.20x + 0.30(x - 300)$
C) $R(x) = 0.20(300) + 0.30x$
D) $R(x) = 0.20(300) + 0.30(x - 300)$

(Setting Up Linear Expressions)

Solution by picking a number: Let's choose a value for x, say $x = 305$. The songwriter gets paid $0.20 per download for the first 300 downloads giving $0.20(300) = \$60$. The songwriter gets $0.30 for the last 5 downloads giving $0.30(5) = \$1.50$. So, the songwriter's total royalty payment is $60 + 1.50 = \boxed{61.50}$ dollars.

We now substitute $x = 305$ into each answer choice.

A) $0.20(305) + 0.30(305) = 152.50$
B) $0.20(305) + 0.30(305 - 300) = 62.50$
C) $0.20(300) + 0.30(305) = 151.50$
D) $0.20(300) + 0.30(305 - 300) = 61.50$

Since choice A, B, and C came out incorrect we can eliminate them and the answer is choice **D**.

Notes: (1) D is **not** the correct answer simply because it is equal to 61.50. It is correct because all three of the other choices are **not** 61.50. **You must check all four choices!**

(2) All the above computations can be done in a single step with your calculator (if a calculator is allowed for this problem).

* Algebraic solution: The songwriter's royalty for the first 300 downloads is $0.20(300)$ dollars. The remaining number of downloads is $x - 300$, and the royalty for these is $0.30(x - 300)$ dollars. So, the songwriter's total royalty payment, in dollars, is $0.20(300) + 0.30(x - 300)$. This is choice **D**.

131. In the xy-plane, the point with coordinates (a, b) lies on the line with equation $x - y = k$, where k is a constant. The point with coordinates $(3a, 4b)$ lies on the line with equation $2x - 3y = k$. If $b \neq 0$, what is the value of $\frac{a}{b}$?

   A) $\frac{5}{13}$
   B) $\frac{5}{11}$
   C) $\frac{11}{5}$
   D) $\frac{13}{5}$

(Equations of Lines and Their Graphs)

* Since the point (a, b) lies on the line with equation $x - y = k$, we have $a - b = k$. Since the point $(3a, 4b)$ lies on the line with equation $2x - 3y = k$, we have $2(3a) - 3(4b) = k$. The last equation is equivalent to $6a - 12b = k$. We now have two expressions equal to k, and therefore, these expressions are equal to each other. So, $a - b = 6a - 12b$. We subtract a from each side of the equation and we add $12b$ to each side of the equation to get $11b = 5a$. We now divide each side of the equation by $5b$ to get $\frac{11}{5} = \frac{a}{b}$. So, the answer is choice **C**.

132. A teacher has c calculators in her classroom, one-third of which are broken. After throwing away the broken calculators, she orders 5 new packs of calculators, each pack containing 3 calculators. After the new calculators are delivered, she now has k calculators. Which of the following equations gives c in terms of k ?

    A) $c = \frac{2k+45}{3}$
    B) $c = \frac{3k-45}{2}$
    C) $c = \frac{k-45}{6}$
    D) $c = \frac{2k}{3} + 30$

(Manipulating Linear Expressions)

* Algebraic solution: The number of broken calculators is $\frac{1}{3}c$ and the number of calculators ordered is $5 \cdot 3 = 15$. So, once the new calculators are delivered, the teacher has $k = c - \frac{1}{3}c + 15 = \frac{2}{3}c + 15$ calculators.

We now solve this equation for c. We first subtract 15 from each side of the equation to get $k - 15 = \frac{2}{3}c$. We multiply each side of this equation by $\frac{3}{2}$ to get $c = \frac{3}{2}(k - 15) = \frac{3(k-15)}{2} = \frac{3k-45}{2}$, choice **B**.

Note: This problem can also be solved by picking a number. I leave the details of this solution to the reader.

133. An ornithologist captures birds, tags them, and then releases them into the wild. Albatrosses are tagged with a plastic tag weighting 0.4 pounds, whereas eagles are tagged with a metal tag weighing 1.1 pounds. The ornithologist's goal last year was to tag 7500 birds. Although he did not meet his goal, he did use up more than 5120 pounds of tags. Which of the following systems of inequalities describes a, the possible number albatrosses that were tagged and e, the possible number of eagles that were tagged?

    A) $a + e < 7500$
       $0.4a + 1.1e < 5120$
    B) $a + e < 7500$
       $0.4a + 1.1e > 5120$
    C) $a + e > 7500$
       $0.4a + 1.1e < 5120$
    D) $a + e > 7500$
       $0.4a + 1.1e > 5120$

(Setting Up Linear Systems)

* The total number of birds tagged was $a + e$. If the ornithologist had met his goal, then we would have $a + e \geq 7500$. However, he did NOT meet his goal, and so we have $a + e < 7500$. This narrows down the answer to either choice A or B.

The total weight of the plastic tags, in pounds, is $0.4a$ and the total weight of the metal tags, in pounds, is $1.1e$. So, the total weight, in pounds, of all tags is $0.4a + 1.1e$. We are told that this value is more than 5120. Therefore, we have $0.4a + 1.1e > 5120$, and the answer is choice **B**.

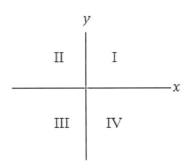

134. If the system of inequalities $x + 2y > 5$ and $3y \le x$ is graphed in the xy-plane above, which quadrants contain solutions to the system?

    A) I only
    B) II and III only
    C) I and IV only
    D) I, II, III, and IV

(Advanced Linear Systems)

* Complete algebraic solution: Let's sketch each inequality, one at a time, starting with $x + 2y > 5$. We first sketch the line $x + 2y = 5$ by plotting the two intercepts. We get the y-intercept by setting $x = 0$. In this case we get $2y = 5$, or equivalently, $y = 2.5$. So, the point $(0, 2.5)$ is on the line. We get the x-intercept by setting $y = 0$. In this case we get $x = 5$, so that the point $(5, 0)$ is on the line. This line is shown in the figure on the left below. Note that we draw a dotted line because the strict inequality $>$ tells us that points on this line are not actually solutions to the inequality $x + 2y > 5$.

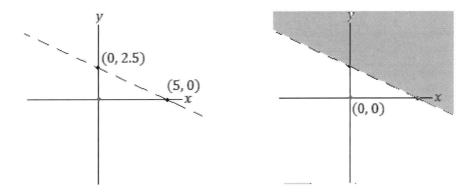

Now we need to figure out which direction to shade. To do this we plug any point *not on the line* into the inequality. For example, we can use $(0, 0)$. Substituting this point into $x + 2y > 5$ gives $0 > 5$. Since this expression is false, we shade the region that does NOT include $(0, 0)$ as shown above in the figure on the right.

We now do the same thing for the inequality $3y \leq x$. The only intercept of $3y = x$ is $(0,0)$. We should plot one more point. If we set $y = 1$, we get $x = 3$. So, the point $(3,1)$ is on the line. We cannot use $(0,0)$ as a test point because it lies on the line. Let's use $(0,1)$ instead. When we test $(0,1)$ we get the false statement $3 \leq 0$.

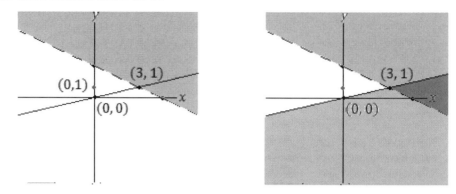

The figure on the above left shows the graph of $3y = x$ with the points $(0,0)$ and $(3,1)$ plotted, as well as the test point $(0,1)$, and the graph on the right shows three different shadings. The middle right shading is the solution set of the given system.

Note that there are solutions in quadrants I and IV only, choice **C**.

$$5k - \frac{1}{3}m = 10$$
$$3k - 2m = 18$$

135. If (k, m) is the unique solution to the system of linear equations above, what is the value of $|m|$?

(Solving Linear Systems of Equations)

* Solution using the elimination method: Let's first multiply each side of the first equation by 3 to get rid of the denominator. The first equation then becomes $15k - m = 30$.

We now multiply each side of the second equation by -5 and add the two equations.

$$15k - m = 30$$
$$\underline{-15k + 10m = -90}$$
$$9m = -60$$

So, $m = -\frac{60}{9} = -\frac{20}{3}$. It follows that $|m| = \mathbf{20/3}$ or $\mathbf{6.66}$ or $\mathbf{6.67}$.

136. A carpenter spent a total of \$5.44 for nails and screws. Each screw cost 2 times as much as each nail, and the carpenter bought 6 times as many nails as screws. How much, in dollars, did the carpenter spend on screws? (Disregard the \$ sign when gridding your answer.)

(Solving Linear Systems of Equations)

* Solution by guessing and picking a number: Let's assume that the carpenter bought 1 screw. It follows that the carpenter bought 6 nails. By guessing and checking we find that each nail is $0.68 and therefore the screw is $2(0.68) = \$1.36$ (check: $6(0.68) + 1.36 = 5.44$). So, we grid in **1.36**.

Note: If we let s be the cost of the screw, we can formally find the cost of the screw by solving the following equation: $s + 6(\frac{s}{2}) = 5.44$. In this case, we have $4s = 5.44$, so that $s = \frac{5.44}{4} = 1.36$.

Algebraic solution: Let s be the number of screws the carpenter bought and c the cost for each screw. It follows that the carpenter bought $6s$ nails and the cost of each nail was $\frac{1}{2}c$. Since the total spent was $5.44, we have $cs + \frac{1}{2}c \cdot 6s = 5.44$, or equivalently, $4cs = 5.44$. Dividing each side of this equation by 4 gives us $cs = 1.36$. But, cs is the cost for each screw times the number of screws. In other words, cs is the amount, in dollars, that the carpenter spent on screws. So, we grid in **1.36**.

LEVEL 5: PASSPORT TO ADVANCED MATH

137. The expression $\frac{x^2}{5} - 1$ can be written as $\frac{1}{5}(x + a)(x - a)$, where a is a positive real number. What is the value of a ?

   A) 1
   B) $\sqrt{5}$
   C) 5
   D) 25

(Factoring)

* $\frac{x^2}{5} - 1 = \frac{1}{5}(x^2 - 5) = \frac{1}{5}(x + \sqrt{5})(x - \sqrt{5})$. So, $a = \sqrt{5}$, choice **B**.

Alternate solution: $\frac{1}{5}(x + a)(x - a) = \frac{1}{5}(x^2 - a^2) = \frac{x^2}{5} - \frac{a^2}{5}$. So, we must have $\frac{a^2}{5} = 1$, or equivalently, $a^2 = 5$. So, $a = \pm\sqrt{5}$. Since we are given that a is positive, $a = \sqrt{5}$, choice **B**.

$$f(x) = (x - a)^2(x - b)^3(x - c)$$

138. In the function $f(x)$ defined above, a, b, and c are constants with $a < 0$, $b < 0$, and $c > 0$. Which of the following could be the graph of f ?

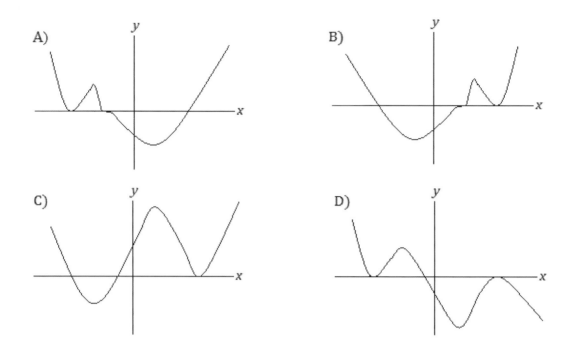

(Graphs of Functions)

* Since a and b are negative, there are two negative zeros. This means that there are two x-intercepts to the left of the y-axis, and we can eliminate choice B.

One of the negative zeros is a double zero. The graph does NOT pass through the x-axis at a double zero. This eliminates choice C.

$c > 0$ is a zero of multiplicity 1 to the right of the y-axis. So, the graph DOES pass through the x-axis at $x = c$. This eliminates choice D. The answer, therefore, is choice **A**.

Notes: (1) A **polynomial** has the form $a_n x^n + a_{n-1} x^{n-1} + \cdots + a_1 x + a_0$ where a_0, $a_1,...,a_n$ are real numbers. For example, $x^2 + 2x - 35$ is a polynomial. The **degree** of the polynomial is n. In other words, it is the highest power that appears in the expanded form of the polynomial.

(2) If a polynomial is in factored form, then we can get the degree of the polynomial by adding the degrees of the factors. For example, the polynomial $f(x) = (x - a)^2(x - b)^3(x - c)$ given in this problem has degree $2 + 3 + 1 = 6$.

(3) Whether the polynomial has even or odd degree can tell us about the polynomial's "end behavior." If the polynomial has even degree, then both ends of the graph head in the same direction (both up to ∞, or both down to $-\infty$). If the polynomial has odd degree, then the ends of the graph head in different directions (one up and the other down)

Since the polynomial in this problem has even degree (degree 6) both ends of the graph head in the same direction, and we can eliminate choice D.

(4) r is a **zero** of a polynomial $p(x)$ if $p(r) = 0$, and the Factor Theorem tells us that r is a zero of a polynomial if and only if $x - r$ is a factor of the polynomial. The zeros of the polynomial in this problem are a, b, and c.

(5) The multiplicity of the zero r is the degree of the factor $x - r$. In this problem, a has multiplicity 2, b has multiplicity 3, and c has multiplicity 1.

(6) A zero r of a polynomial has odd multiplicity if and only if the graph of the polynomial passes through the x-axis at $x = r$. So, the graph of the polynomial in this problem must pass through the x-axis at $x = b$ and $x = c$.

(7) A zero r of a polynomial has even multiplicity if and only if the graph of the polynomial touches the x-axis at $x = r$, but does not pass through it. So, the graph of the polynomial in this problem does NOT pass through the x-axis at $x = a$.

139. Which of the following is equivalent to $\dfrac{3x^2 + 7x - 3}{3x + 1}$?

A) $x + \dfrac{7}{3}$

B) $x + \dfrac{7}{3} - \dfrac{3}{x}$

C) $x + 1 - \dfrac{5}{3x+1}$

D) $x + 2 - \dfrac{5}{3x+1}$

(Operations on Polynomials)

* Solution using synthetic division: We first factor out the 3 in the denominator to get

$$\frac{3x^2 + 7x - 3}{3\left(x + \frac{1}{3}\right)} = \frac{1}{3} \cdot \frac{3x^2 + 7x - 3}{x + \frac{1}{3}}$$

We now use synthetic division to divide $3x^2 + 7x - 3$ by $x + \dfrac{1}{3}$

$$
\begin{array}{r|rrr}
-\frac{1}{3} & 3 & 7 & -3 \\
 & & -1 & -2 \\
\hline
 & 3 & 6 & -5
\end{array}
$$

So,

$$\frac{3x^2 + 7x - 3}{x + \frac{1}{3}} = 3x + 6 - \frac{5}{x + \frac{1}{3}}$$

And finally, we have

$$\frac{3x^2 + 7x - 3}{3x + 1} = \frac{1}{3} \cdot \frac{3x^2 + 7x - 3}{x + \frac{1}{3}} = \frac{1}{3}\left(3x + 6 - \frac{5}{x + \frac{1}{3}}\right) = x + 2 - \frac{5}{3x + 1}$$

This is choice **D**.

Notes: (1) We can use a procedure called **synthetic division** whenever we divide any polynomial by a linear polynomial of the form $x - r$.

If we are dividing by $x - r$, then we begin by writing r in the upper left-hand corner. In this problem, we are dividing $3x^2 + 7x - 3$ by $x + \frac{1}{3} = x - (-\frac{1}{3})$. So, $r = -\frac{1}{3}$.

Next, we make sure that the polynomial we are dividing is written in descending order of exponents (which it is) and that every exponent is accounted for (which they are). We then write down the coefficients of this polynomial. So, we have the following:

$$-\tfrac{1}{3}\big|\quad 3 \quad 7 \quad -3$$

We begin by bringing down the 3.

$$-\tfrac{1}{3}\big|\quad 3 \quad 7 \quad -3$$
$$\overline{ 3 }$$

We now multiply this number by the number in the upper left. So, we have $(3)\left(-\frac{1}{3}\right) = -1$. We place this number under the 7.

$$-\tfrac{1}{3}\big|\quad 3 \quad 7 \quad -3$$
$$\underline{ -1 }$$
$$3$$

Next, we add 7 and -1 to get 6.

$$-\tfrac{1}{3}\big|\quad 3 \quad 7 \quad -3$$
$$\underline{ -1 }$$
$$3 \quad 6$$

Again, we multiply this number by the number in the upper left. So, we have $(6)\left(-\frac{1}{3}\right) = -2$. We place this number under the -3.

$$-\tfrac{1}{3}\big|\quad 3 \quad 7 \quad -3$$
$$\underline{ -1 \quad -2}$$
$$3 \quad 6$$

Finally, we add -3 and -2 to get -5.

$$-\tfrac{1}{3}\rfloor \quad 3 \quad 7 \quad -3$$
$$\underline{\qquad\qquad -1 \quad -2\quad}$$
$$\qquad\quad 3 \quad 6 \quad -5$$

The bottom row gives the coefficients of the quotient (which is a polynomial of 1 degree less than the dividend) and the remainder.

So, the quotient polynomial is $3x + 6$ and the remainder is -5.

We put the remainder over the linear divisor and add it to the quotient.

So, we have $\dfrac{3x^2+7x-3}{x+\frac{1}{3}} = 3x + 6 + \dfrac{-5}{x+\frac{1}{3}} = 3x + 6 - \dfrac{5}{x+\frac{1}{3}}$.

(2) Synthetic division can be used only when dividing by an expression of the form $x - r$. In this problem, the divisor we are given is $3x + 1$. We fix this issue by factoring 3 from this expression to get $3\left(x + \frac{1}{3}\right)$.

Factoring out this 3 in the denominator is equivalent to factoring $\frac{1}{3}$ out of the whole expression.

(3) We then proceed to synthetically divide $3x^2 + 7x - 3$ by $x + \frac{1}{3}$ to get $3x + 6 - \dfrac{5}{x+\frac{1}{3}}$.

At the end, we multiply this last result by $\frac{1}{3}$ to get the final answer.

(4) Observe how the distributive property was used twice to get the final result. The first time is when we initially distribute $\frac{1}{3}$ to each of the three terms (first step below), and the second time is when we distribute the 3 in the denominator (last step below).

$$\frac{1}{3}\left(3x + 6 - \frac{5}{x+\frac{1}{3}}\right) = \frac{1}{3}\cdot 3x + \frac{1}{3}\cdot 6 - \frac{1}{3}\left(\frac{5}{x+\frac{1}{3}}\right) = x + 2 - \frac{5}{3\left(x+\frac{1}{3}\right)} = x + 2 - \frac{5}{3x + 1}$$

(5) This problem can also be solved using long division. This procedure is more time consuming than synthetic division, so I will omit it here and leave it as an optional exercise for the interested reader.

140. If $\dfrac{7^{k^2}}{7^{m^2}} = 7^{10}$ and $k - m = 5$, what is the value of $k + m$?

    A) 1
    B) 2
    C) 5
    D) 10

(Exponents and Roots and Factoring)

* $\frac{7^{k^2}}{7^{m^2}} = 7^{k^2-m^2}$. So, $k^2 - m^2 = 10$. Also, $k^2 - m^2 = (k-m)(k+m)$. So, $10 = 5(k+m)$, and therefore, $k + m = \frac{10}{5} = 2$, choice **B**.

141. Two different points on a number line are both 7 units from the point with coordinate -5. The solution to which of the following equations gives the coordinates of both points?

    A) $|x + 5| = 7$
    B) $|x - 5| = 7$
    C) $|x + 7| = 5$
    D) $|x - 7| = 5$

(Manipulating Nonlinear Expressions)

* Geometrically, $|x - y|$ is the distance between x and y. In this question, we are given that the distance between x and -5 is 7. So, $|x - (-5)| = 7$, or equivalently, $|x + 5| = 7$, choice **A**.

Notes: (1) It's not hard to check if we chose the correct answer by plugging in a number. Let's think of a point that is 7 units from -5. Well, how about the number 2. Since 2 is 7 units away from -5, it should satisfy the equation. Let's check: $|x + 5| = |2 + 5| = |7| = 7$. This works, and so it looks like we picked the right choice.

(2) The other point that is 7 units from -5 is -12. Let's check that this one works too: $|x + 5| = |-12 + 5| = |-7| = 7$. Yep! This one works too.

(3) Below is a picture showing the points -5, 2, and -12, and that the two distances are 7.

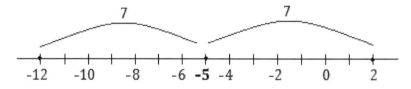

142. If $c^{\frac{d}{3}} = 16$ for positive integers c and d, what is a possible value of cd ?

(Exponents and Roots)

* $c = 16^{\frac{3}{d}}$. If we let $d = 1$, we get $c = 16^3 = 4096$. So, $cd = 4096 \cdot 1 = \textbf{4096}$.

Note: We can also let d be 2, 3, 4, 6, or 12, to get $c = 64, 16, 8, 4,$ and 2, respectively. Thus, the possible values of cd are 4096, 128, 48, 32, and 24.

143. If $(2x + a)(dx + b) = 6x^2 + 29x + c$ for all values of x, and $a + b = 13$, what is the value of c ?

(Solving Quadratic Equations)

* We need $2d = 6$. So, $d = 3$. We now have

$$(2x + a)(3x + b) = 6x^2 + 29x + c$$

We need $2b + 3a = 29$.

We can now either use trial and error or formally solve the following system of equations:

$$3a + 2b = 29$$
$$a + b = 13$$

We get $a = 3$ and $b = 10$

It follows that $c = ab = 3 \cdot 10 = \mathbf{30}$.

Notes: (1) $(2x + a)(dx + b) = 2dx^2 + (2b + ad)x + ab$

(2) Using Note (1), we have

$$2dx^2 + (2b + ad)x + ab = 6x^2 + 29x + c$$

(3) using Note (2) and equating coefficients of each power of x, we have

$$2d = 6 \qquad\qquad 2b + ad = 29 \qquad\qquad ab = c$$

(4) The first equation in Note (3) gives us $d = \frac{6}{2} = 3$.

(5) Substituting $d = 3$ into the second equation gives us $2b + 3a = 29$.

(6) We can solve the system of equations that appears in the solution formally using the elimination method. We can start by multiplying each side of the second equation by -2.

$$3a + 2b = 29$$
$$-2(a + b) = 13(-2)$$

We now distribute the -2 on the left, and add the two equations.

$$\begin{array}{rcr} 3a + 2b = & 29 \\ -2a - 2b = & -26 \\ \hline a = & 3 \end{array}$$

Since $a + b = 13$, we must have $b = 13 - a = 13 - 3 = 10$.

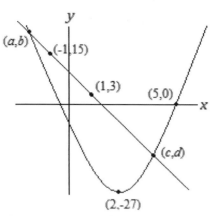

144. The xy-plane above shows the two points of intersection of the graphs of a linear function and a quadratic function. The leftmost point of intersection has coordinates (a, b) and the rightmost point of intersection has coordinates (c, d). If the vertex of the graph of the quadratic function is at $(2, -27)$, what is the value of $b - d$?

(Graphs of Parabolas and Nonlinear Systems of Equations)

* Algebraic solution: The standard form of the quadratic function is $y = p(x - 2)^2 - 27$ for some real number p. Since $(5, 0)$ is on the parabola, we have $0 = p(5 - 2)^2 - 27 = 9p - 27$. So, $9p = 27$, and therefore, $p = \frac{27}{9} = 3$. So, the quadratic function is $y = 3(x - 2)^2 - 27$.

The slope of the line is $m = \frac{3-15}{1-(-1)} = \frac{-12}{2} = -6$. So, an equation of the line in point-slope form is $y - 3 = -6(x - 1)$. We solve this equation for y to get $y = -6x + 9$.

To find the points of intersection of the parabola and the line we must solve the system of equations

$$y = 3(x - 2)^2 - 27$$
$$y = -6x + 9$$

Substituting $-6x + 9$ in for y in the first equation gives

$$-6x + 9 = 3(x - 2)^2 - 27$$
$$-6x + 9 = 3(x - 2)(x - 2) - 27$$
$$-6x + 9 = 3(x^2 - 4x + 4) - 27$$
$$-6x + 9 = 3x^2 - 12x + 12 - 27$$
$$0 = 3x^2 - 6x - 24$$
$$0 = x^2 - 2x - 8$$
$$0 = (x - 4)(x + 2)$$
$$x - 4 = 0 \qquad x + 2 = 0$$
$$x = 4 \qquad x = -2$$

When $x = 4$, we have $y = -6 \cdot 4 + 9 = -24 + 9 = -15$.

When $x = -2$, we have $y = (-6)(-2) + 9 = 12 + 9 = 21$.

So $(a, b) = (-2, 21)$ and $(c, d) = (4, -15)$.

In particular, $b = 21$, $d = -15$, and so $b - d = 21 - (-15) = 21 + 15 = \textbf{36}$.

Notes: (1) The **standard form** for the equation of a parabola is

$$y = p(x - h)^2 + k, \text{ or equivalently, } y - k = p(x - h)^2$$

In either of these forms, we can identify the vertex of the parabola as (h, k).

In this problem, we are given that the vertex is $(2, -27)$. So, $h = 2$ and $k = -27$.

(2) Once we know h and k, we can find p by plugging any point on the parabola (except the vertex) into the equation and solving for p.

In this problem, we used the point $(5, 0)$.

(3) Recall that the slope of a line passing through the points (x_1, y_1) and (x_2, y_2) is

$$\text{Slope} = m = \frac{\text{rise}}{\text{run}} = \frac{y_2 - y_1}{x_2 - x_1}$$

In this problem, we used the points $(-1, 15)$ and $(1, 3)$.

(4) The **slope-intercept form of an equation of a line** is $y = mx + b$ where m is the slope of the line and b is the y-coordinate of the y-intercept, i.e. the point $(0, b)$ is on the line. Note that this point lies on the y-axis.

It turned out that $m = -6$ and $b = 9$

(5) The **point-slope form of an equation of a line** is

$$y - y_0 = m(x - x_0)$$

where m is the slope of the line and (x_0, y_0) is any point on the line.

In this problem, $m = -6$ and $(x_0, y_0) = (1, 3)$.

(6) We could have used the point $(-1, 15)$ instead when writing an equation of the line in point-slope form. In this case, we would get $y - 15 = -6(x + 1)$. I leave it to the reader to show that when you solve this equation for y you get the same slope-intercept form as before.

(7) As an alternative to using point-slope form, after finding m, we could plug one of the points into the slope-intercept form of the equation and solve for b as follows:

$$y = -6x + b$$
$$3 = -6(1) + b$$
$$3 = -6 + b$$
$$b = 3 + 6 = 9$$

(8) If a calculator is allowed for this problem we could solve the system

$$y = 3(x - 2)^2 - 27$$
$$y = -6x + 9$$

by entering these graphs into our calculator and using the "intersect" feature. I leave this method as an exercise for the reader.

LEVEL 5: PROBLEM SOLVING

145. In physics, the force F acting on an object of mass m yields an acceleration a, and this relationship can be expressed by the formula $F = ma$. Furthermore, the amount of work done by this force can be expressed using the formula $W = Fd$, where d is the distance of the object from its starting point. If mass is measured in kilograms (kg), acceleration is measured in meters per second square, (m/s^2), distance is measured in meters (m), force is measured in Newtons (N), and work is measured in Joules (J), which of the following units could be used to represent work?

I. kg m^2/s^2
II. m^2/N
III. N · m

A) II only
B) III only
C) I and III only
D) I, II and III

(Ratios)

* F is measured in Newtons (N) and d is measured in meters (m). It follows that $W = Fd$ can be measured in N · m. Therefore, III works, and we can eliminate choice A.

Now, m is measured in kilograms (kg) and a is measured in meters per second squared (m/s^2). It follows that F can be measured in kg m/s^2 (i.e., $1\,N = 1\,kg\,m/s^2$). So, W can be measured in (kg m/s^2) · m = kg m^2/s^2. Therefore, I works, and we can eliminate choice B.

Now for II, we have m^2/N = m^2 ÷ kg m/s^2 = m^2 · s^2/(kg · m) = m s^2/kg. Since this is not equal to kg m^2/s^2, II does not work, and the answer is choice **C**.

$$\frac{1}{x^3}, \frac{1}{x^2}, \frac{1}{x}, x^2, x^3$$

146. If $-1 < x < 0$, what is the median of the five numbers in the list above?

A) $\frac{1}{x^3}$
B) $\frac{1}{x^2}$
C) $\frac{1}{x}$
D) x^3

* **Solution by picking a number:** Let's choose $x = -\frac{1}{2}$.

Then we have $\frac{1}{x^3} = (-2)^3 = -8, \frac{1}{x^2} = (-2)^2 = 4, \frac{1}{x} = -2, x^2 = \frac{1}{4}$ and $x^3 = \left(-\frac{1}{2}\right)^3 = -\frac{1}{8}$.

Now let's place them in increasing order.

$$-8, -2, -\frac{1}{8}, \frac{1}{4}, 4$$

The median is $-\frac{1}{8}$ which is x^3, choice **D**.

Note: If we are allowed to use a calculator for this problem, we can do all the computations in our calculator and get the following decimals:

$$\frac{1}{x^3} = -8 \quad \frac{1}{x^2} = 4 \quad \frac{1}{x} = -2 \quad x^2 = 0.25 \quad x^3 = -0.125$$

Here they are in increasing order:

$$-8, -2, -0.125, 0.25, 4$$

The median is -0.125 which is x^3, choice D.

147. A chef in Japan conducted an experiment to determine if choice in utensils affects how people rate the quality of a meal. The same meal was served to a group of volunteers. Half of the volunteers were given forks and the other half were given chopsticks. The chef concluded that the average rating of the quality of the meal was significantly higher for those that were given chopsticks. Based upon this experiment, which of the following statements is the most accurate?

   A) The choice of utensils was the cause of the difference in the average rating of the quality of the meal, but it is not reasonable to generalize this conclusion to all people from Japan.
   B) The choice of utensils was the cause of the difference in the average rating of the quality of the meal, and this conclusion can be generalized to all people from Japan.
   C) It is not possible to draw any conclusion from this experiment because volunteers were used.
   D) It is not reasonable to conclude that the choice of utensils was the cause in the difference in the average rating of the quality of the meal for these volunteers.

(Data Analysis)

* The population mentioned in this problem consists of volunteers. Therefore, the results can be generalized only to volunteers. So, we can eliminate choice B.

Since the choice of utensils is the only variable in the experiment, it is reasonable to conclude that the choice of utensils was the cause of the difference in the average rating of the quality of the meal. So, we can eliminate choices C and D, and the answer is choice **A**.

Note: Don't change the population. The results from one population DO NOT carry over to another population.

Choice B mentions "all people from Japan." This is a different population than "volunteers." Since results from one population do not carry over to another population, we can eliminate choice B.

Questions 148 - 150 refer to the following information.

A ball is launched into the air and the height of the ball, in feet, is estimated $\frac{1}{2}$ second after it is launched. The ball is then launched again and this time the height of the ball is estimated 1 second after it is launched. This experiment is repeated 16 times, and on the nth launch, the height of the ball is estimated $\frac{n}{2}$ seconds after it is launched. The results are shown in the scatterplot below and a quadratic model that best fits the data is also shown.

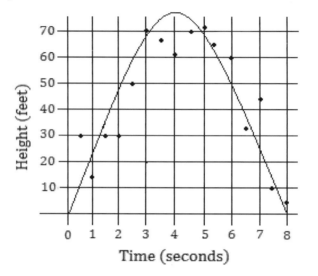

148. Let a be the number of times the model predicts that the height of a launched ball will be exactly 8 feet and let b be the number of times the estimated height of the launched ball was 8 feet. What is the value of $a + b$?

    A) 0
    B) 1
    C) 2
    D) 3

(Scatterplots)

* We draw a horizontal line at a height of 8 feet (as shown in the picture on the right).

The horizontal line hits the graph of the quadratic model two times, so that $a = 2$.

The horizontal line does not hit any data points, so that $b = 0$.

It follows that $a + b = 2 + 0 = 2$, choice **C**.

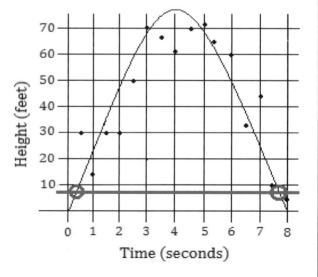

149. For what fraction of the 16 launches is the estimated height an underestimate as compared to the height predicted by the model?

A) $\frac{9}{16}$

B) $\frac{1}{2}$

C) $\frac{7}{16}$

D) $\frac{3}{8}$

(Scatterplots)

* The estimated height is an underestimate as compared to the height predicted by the model if the data point corresponding to the estimated height is *below* the quadratic graph. All these data points are in the shaded region shown in the picture on the right. There are 9 of these data points out of a total of 16 data points. So, the answer is $\frac{9}{16}$, choice **A**.

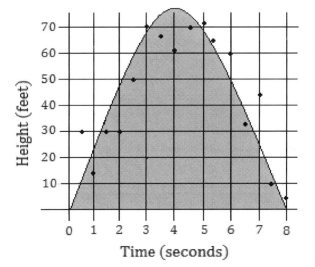

150. For the twelfth launch, which of the following best approximates the percent decrease from the estimated height to the height that the model predicts?

A) 12%

B) $16\frac{2}{3}\%$

C) 20%

D) $24\frac{1}{3}\%$

(Scatterplots and Percents)

* When $n = 12$, $t = \frac{12}{2} = 6$, the estimated height is 60 feet, and the height that the model predicts is 50 feet. We now use the percent change formula

$$\text{Percent Change} = \frac{\text{Change}}{\text{Original}} \times 100$$

Here the Original value is 60 and the Change is $60 - 50 = 10$.

It follows that $\text{Percent Change} = \frac{10}{60} \times 100 = \frac{50}{3}\% = 16\frac{2}{3}\%$, choice **B**.

151. A child starts coloring with a crayon that is 3.5 inches in length. As the child colors, the length of the crayon is decreasing at a constant rate. After 2 minutes, 20% of the crayon has been used. Which of the following equations models the length of crayon, c, still remaining t minutes after the child started coloring?

    A) $c = 3.5 - 2t$
    B) $c = 3.5 - 0.35t$
    C) $c = 3.5(0.2)^{\frac{t}{2}}$
    D) $c = 3.5(0.8)^{\frac{t}{2}}$

(Growth)

* Since the length is decreasing "at a constant rate," the relationship is linear. Since the relationships in choices C and D are exponential, we can eliminate choices C and D.

Since 20% of the crayon is used after 2 minutes, 80% of the crayon is remaining after 2 minutes. Now, 80% of 3.5 is $0.8 \cdot 3.5 = 2.8$. It follows, that when $t = 2$, $c = 2.8$. Let's substitute $t = 2$ into choices A and B.

    A) $c = 3.5 - 2 \cdot 2 = 3.5 - 4 = -0.5$
    B) $c = 3.5 - 0.35 \cdot 2 = 3.5 - 0.7 = 2.8$

Since choice A came out incorrect, we can eliminate it, and the answer is choice **B**.

Notes: (1) A relationship is linear if it changes by a constant amount (or changes at a constant rate) and a relationship is exponential if it changes by a constant percentage.

(2) Observe that if we substitute $t = 2$ into choice D, we get $c = 3.5(0.8)^{\frac{2}{2}} = 3.5 \cdot 0.8 = 2.8$. So, if the second sentence was not given in the problem, choice D would be an acceptable answer as well. Also, if we were to change the second sentence to "As the child colors, the length of the crayon is decreasing at a constant percentage," then the answer would be choice D instead of choice B.

152. A group of students take a test and the average score is 90. One more student takes the test and receives a score of 81 decreasing the average score of the group to 87. How many students were in the initial group?

(Statistics)

* **Solution by changing averages to sums:** We use the formula

Sum = Average · Number

Let n be the number of students in the group. Then originally the sum of the test scores was $90n$.

When the new student takes the test, the number of students is $n + 1$, and the sum of the test scores is $87(n + 1) = 87n + 87$.

So, we have

$$90n + 81 = 87n + 87$$
$$3n = 6$$
$$n = \mathbf{2}.$$

LEVEL 5: GEOMETRY AND COMPLEX NUMBERS

153. Samantha, Janice, and Christina are standing so that the distance between Samantha and Janice is 15 feet and the distance between Janice and Christina is 9 feet. Which of the following could be the distance between Samantha and Christina?

   I. 6 feet
  II. 17 feet
 III. 24 feet

    A) I only
    B) II only
    C) I and III only
    D) I, II, and III

(Triangles)

* Solution using the triangle inequality: The **triangle inequality** says that the length of the third side of a triangle is between the sum and difference of the lengths of the other two sides.

In this problem, there are two cases to consider:

<u>Case 1</u> **(Samantha, Janice, and Christina are standing on the vertices of a triangle):** In this case, we use the triangle inequality to get that the distance between Samantha and Christina is between $15 - 9 = 6$ and $15 + 9 = 24$. So, 17 feet is a possible distance between Samantha and Christina, and we can eliminate choices A and C.

<u>Case 2</u> **(Samantha, Janice, and Christina are standing in a straight line):** In this case, the distance between Samantha and Christina is either $15 - 9 = 6$ or $15 + 9 = 24$. So, 6 feet and 24 feet are also possible distances between Samantha and Christina. Therefore, the answer is choice **D**.

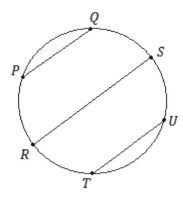

154. In the circle above with diameter d, chords $\overline{PQ}$ and $\overline{TU}$ are parallel to diameter $\overline{RS}$. If $\overline{PQ}$ and $\overline{TU}$ are each $\frac{3}{4}$ of the length of $\overline{RS}$, what is the distance between chords $\overline{PQ}$ and $\overline{TU}$ in terms of d ?

    A) $\frac{d\sqrt{7}}{8}$

    B) $\frac{d\sqrt{7}}{4}$

    C) $\frac{\pi d}{4}$

    D) $\frac{3\pi d}{4}$

(Circles)

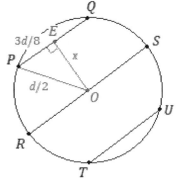

* Let's add some information to the picture. We draw segments $\overline{OP}$ and $\overline{OE}$ to form triangle OEP. Since the circle has diameter d, the radius of the circle is $\frac{d}{2}$. Note that $\overline{OP}$ is a radius of the circle and therefore has length $\frac{d}{2}$. Now, we are given $PQ = \frac{3}{4}d$ so that $PE = \frac{1}{2}PQ = \frac{1}{2}\left(\frac{3}{4}d\right) = \frac{3d}{8}$.

We now use the Pythagorean Theorem to find x:

$$\left(\tfrac{d}{2}\right)^2 = x^2 + \left(\tfrac{3d}{8}\right)^2$$

$$\frac{d^2}{4} = x^2 + \frac{9d^2}{64}$$

$$x^2 = \frac{d^2}{4} - \frac{9d^2}{64} = \frac{16d^2}{16\cdot4} - \frac{9d^2}{64} = \frac{16d^2 - 9d^2}{64} = \frac{7d^2}{64}$$

So $OE = x = \frac{\sqrt{7}d}{8} = \frac{d\sqrt{7}}{8}$.

It follows that the distance between $\overline{PQ}$ and $\overline{TU}$ is $2OE = 2\cdot\frac{d\sqrt{7}}{8} = \frac{d\sqrt{7}}{4}$, choice **B**.

Notes: (1) In problems involving circles, it is often helpful to draw in your own radius. To find a suitable radius, look along the circumference of the circle for "key points." In the given figure, drawing a radius from the center of the circle to any of points $P, Q, T,$ or U would work.

(2) The diameter of a circle is twice the radius, or $d = 2r$. Equivalently, the radius of a circle is half the diameter, or $r = \frac{d}{2}$.

(3) Recall that the Pythagorean Theorem says that if a right triangle has legs of length a and b, and a hypotenuse of length c, then $c^2 = a^2 + b^2$.

Note that the hypotenuse of a right triangle is always opposite the right angle, and the length of the hypotenuse is always by itself in the formula for the Pythagorean Theorem.

In this problem $a = x$, $b = \frac{3d}{8}$, and $c = \frac{d}{2}$.

(4) The distance between two parallel lines (or line segments) is the length of a line segment between the two lines that is perpendicular to both lines.

In this case, the distance between $\overline{PQ}$ and $\overline{TU}$ is $2OE$.

$$SA = s^2 + 2s\sqrt{\left(\frac{s}{2}\right)^2 + h^2}$$

155. The formula above can be used to calculate the total surface area of a pyramid, where h is the height of the pyramid, and s is the length of the square base. What must the expression $s\sqrt{\left(\frac{s}{2}\right)^2 + h^2}$ represent?

    A) The area of the square base
    B) The area of a triangular face
    C) The sum of the areas of two triangular faces
    D) The sum of the areas of all four triangular faces

(Solid Geometry)

* Quick solution: The area of the square base is s^2. Since the surface area of a pyramid consists of the area of the square base plus the sum of the areas of the four triangular faces, it follows that $2s\sqrt{\left(\frac{s}{2}\right)^2 + h^2}$ represents the sum of the areas of all four triangular faces. So, $s\sqrt{\left(\frac{s}{2}\right)^2 + h^2}$ represents the sum of the areas of two triangular faces, choice **C**.

Complete solution: Let's draw the pyramid, the square base and a triangular face.

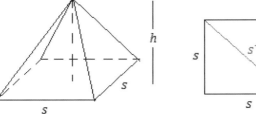
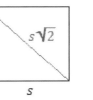
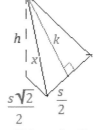

          Pyramid   Square Base   Triangular Face

Observe that the area of the square base is s^2. This eliminates choice A. Also, the length of the diagonal of the square base is $s\sqrt{2}$ (we can get this either by using the Pythagorean Theorem, or by using the fact that the diagonal of a square splits the square into two $45, 45, 90$ right triangles).

Since the diagonal of the square base has length $s\sqrt{2}$, it follows that the distance from the center of the square base to a vertex of the pyramid on the base is $\frac{s\sqrt{2}}{2}$. We can now find the length of a side of a triangular face (labeled x in the rightmost figure above) by applying the Pythagorean Theorem to the triangle with legs of length $\frac{s\sqrt{2}}{2}$ and h. We have $x^2 = h^2 + \left(\frac{s\sqrt{2}}{2}\right)^2 = h^2 + \frac{s^2}{2}$.

We can now find the height of a triangular face by applying the Pythagorean Theorem again. We get $k^2 = x^2 - \left(\frac{s}{2}\right)^2 = h^2 + \frac{s^2}{2} - \frac{s^2}{4} = h^2 + \frac{s^2}{4}$. So $k = \sqrt{\frac{s^2}{4} + h^2} = \sqrt{\left(\frac{s}{2}\right)^2 + h^2}$.

The area of a triangular face is then $\frac{1}{2}sk = \frac{1}{2}s\sqrt{\left(\frac{s}{2}\right)^2 + h^2}$. Since $s\sqrt{\left(\frac{s}{2}\right)^2 + h^2}$ is $2 \cdot \frac{1}{2}s\sqrt{\left(\frac{s}{2}\right)^2 + h^2}$, the expression $s\sqrt{\left(\frac{s}{2}\right)^2 + h^2}$ represents the sum of the areas of two triangular faces, choice **C**.

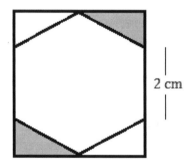

156. The figure above shows a regular hexagon with side length 2 centimeters inscribed in a rectangle. What is the area of the shaded region?

A) $\frac{\sqrt{3}}{2}$
B) $\sqrt{3}$
C) $2\sqrt{3}$
D) 4

(Polygons)

* Since a hexagon has 6 sides, the total number of degrees in the hexagon's interior is $(6 - 2) \cdot 180 = 4 \cdot 180 = 720$. The hexagon is regular, and so each interior angle of the hexagon measures $\frac{720}{6} = 120°$. In the figure on the left, we labeled one of the interior angles of the hexagon with $120°$, and then used supplementary angles to get that one of the angles of the shaded triangle in the upper right of the figure measures $60°$. Since the triangle is a right triangle, it follows that the other angle measures $30°$, as can be seen in the figure on the right. Also, since the hexagon is regular, we can label the hypotenuse of the triangle with 2 cm.

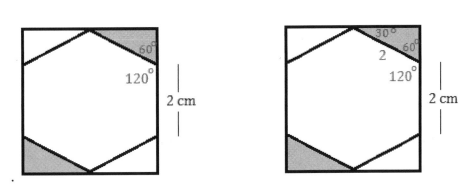

Using the formula for a $30, 60, 90$ triangle, the legs of the triangle have lengths 1 and $\sqrt{3}$. It follows that the area of the triangle is $\frac{1}{2} \cdot 1 \cdot \sqrt{3} = \frac{\sqrt{3}}{2}$. Since there are two shaded triangles, the total area of the shaded region is $2 \cdot \frac{\sqrt{3}}{2} = \sqrt{3}$, choice **B**.

Notes: (1) The total number of degrees in the interior of an n-sided polygon is $(\boldsymbol{n - 2}) \cdot \boldsymbol{180}$.

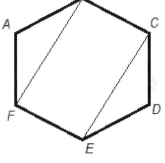

(2) We can also find the total number of degrees in the hexagon's interior by splitting the hexagon up into two triangles and a quadrilateral, as shown in the figure on the right. We then have that the total number of degrees is $180 + 360 + 180 = 720°$.

$$x^2 + y^2 + 8x - 10y - 3 = 0$$

157. The equation above defines a circle in the xy-plane. What are the coordinates of the center of the circle?

    A) $(-4, -5)$
    B) $(-4, 5)$
    C) $(4, -5)$
    D) $(4, 5)$

(Graphs of Circles)

* Solution by completing the square: We add 3 to each side of the equation and complete the square twice on the left-hand side.

$$x^2 + 8x + 16 + y^2 - 10y + 25 = 3 + 16 + 25$$
$$(x + 4)^2 + (y - 5)^2 = 44$$

So, the center of the circle is $(-4, 5)$, choice **B**.

Note: See Problem 108 for more information on completing the square.

119

158. Which of the following is equal to $i^{123} + i^{124} + i^{125} + i^{126}$?

      A) 0
      B) 1
      C) i
      D) $2i$

(Complex Numbers)

* Quick solution: Since 123, 124, 125, and 126 are consecutive integers, i^{123}, i^{124}, i^{125}, and i^{126} are equal to 1, -1, i, and $-i$, not necessarily in that order. So, we have

$$i^{123} + i^{124} + i^{125} + i^{126} = 1 + (-1) + i + (-i) = 0$$

This is choice **A**.

Notes: (1) Recall from Problem 91 that when we raise i to a power we get 1, i, -1, or $-i$, depending upon what the remainder is when we divide the power by 4.

In this solution, we are not saying that i^{123} is equal to 1 (and similarly for the other powers of i). We are saying that one of the four powers of i is equal to 1, one of the powers is equal to -1, and so on. We can say this because the powers of i cycle through these four values.

(2) Since 124 is divisible by 4, $i^{124} = 1$. It follows that $i^{125} = i$, $i^{126} = -1$, and $i^{123} = -i$. So, writing the summand in order, we have $i^{123} + i^{124} + i^{125} + i^{126} = -i + 1 + i + (-1) = 0$

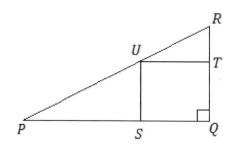

159. In the figure above, ΔPQR is a right triangle, quadrilateral $SUTQ$ is a square, and $PQ = \frac{5}{4}RQ$. The area of the square is what fraction of the area of ΔPQR ?

(Parallel Lines and Similarity)

* Let's let $RQ = x$ and $SQ = y$. Then $PQ = \frac{5}{4}x$, $US = y$, and $PS = PQ - SQ = \frac{5}{4}x - y$.

Using the fact that $\Delta PQR \sim \Delta PSU$, we have $\frac{PQ}{RQ} = \frac{PS}{US}$. So, $\frac{\frac{5}{4}x}{x} = \frac{\frac{5}{4}x-y}{y}$, or equivalently, $\frac{5}{4} = \frac{\frac{5}{4}x-y}{y}$. We cross multiply to get $5y = 4(\frac{5}{4}x - y)$, or equivalently, $5y = 5x - 4y$. So, $9y = 5x$, or equivalently, $y = \frac{5}{9}x$.

Now, the area of the square is $y^2 = \left(\frac{5}{9}x\right)^2 = \frac{25}{81}x^2$ and the area of $\Delta PQR = \frac{1}{2} \cdot \frac{5}{4}x \cdot x = \frac{5}{8}x^2$. So, the desired fraction is $\frac{25}{81}x^2 \div \frac{5}{8}x^2 = \frac{25}{81} \cdot \frac{8}{5} = \frac{40}{81} \approx 0.493827$. So, we can grid in $.493$ or $.494$.

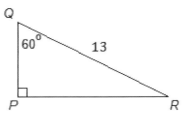

160. In ΔQPR above, point S (not shown) lies on $\overline{QR}$ so that $\overline{PS} \perp \overline{QR}$. What is the value of $\cos(\angle QPS) - \sin(\angle SPR)$?

(Trigonometry)

* Solution using a cofunction identity: Let's add some information to the picture. We draw $\overline{PS}$ so that $\overline{PS} \perp \overline{QR}$. Using the fact that the sum of the measures of the interior angles of a triangle is $180°$ three times (in triangles PRQ, PSQ, and PSR), we get that $m\angle PRQ = 30°$, $m\angle QPS = 30°$, and $m\angle SPR = 60°$.

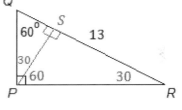

Now, we have $\cos(\angle QPS) - \sin(\angle SPR) = \cos 30° - \sin 60° = \mathbf{0}$.

Notes: (1) We used the cofunction identity $\sin(90° - x) = \cos x$ to get $\sin 60° = \cos 30°$, so that $\cos 30° - \sin 60° = \cos 30° - \cos 30° = 0$.

(2) If you forget the cofunction identities and a calculator is allowed for the problem, then you can simply type $\cos 30° - \sin 60°$ into your calculator to get 0 (make sure your calculator is in degree mode).

(3) If you forget the cofunction identities and a calculator is NOT allowed for the problem, then you can use the special $30, 60, 90$ triangle to compute $\cos 30° = \frac{\sqrt{3}}{2}$ and $\sin 60° = \frac{\sqrt{3}}{2}$.

PROBLEMS BY LEVEL AND TOPIC
PROBLEM SET B

Full solutions to these problems are available for free download here:
www.SATPrepGet800.com/500SATx2

LEVEL 1: HEART OF ALGEBRA

1. For which of the following values of k will the value of $7k - 15$ be greater than 6 ?

   A) 1
   B) 2
   C) 3
   D) 4

2. To rent an economy car, a car rental agency charges $90 per day plus $0.10 per mile. Which of the following gives the cost, $C(x)$, in dollars, of renting an economy car for one day and driving it for x miles?

   A) $C(x) = 90x$
   B) $C(x) = 90x + 0.1$
   C) $C(x) = 0.1x + 90$
   D) $C(x) = 90 - 0.1x$

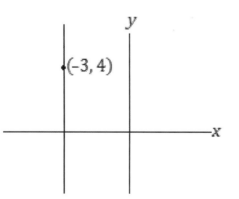

3. The vertical line in the xy-plane shown above passes through the point $(-3, 4)$. Which of the following is an equation for the line?

   A) $x = -3$
   B) $y = -3$
   C) $y = -3x$
   D) $x = -3y$

$$r + g = 25$$

4. The equation above relates the number of red jellybeans, r, and the number of green jellybeans, g, that are in a jar. What does the number 25 represent?

    A) The number of red jellybeans in the jar
    B) The number of green jellybeans in the jar
    C) The total number of jellybeans in the jar
    D) The number of red jellybeans in the jar for each green jellybean in the jar

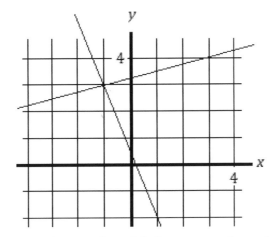

5. The xy-plane above shows the graphs of 2 linear equations. Which of the following ordered pairs (x, y) is the solution to the system defined by these 2 equations?

    A) $(1, 3)$
    B) $(-1, 3)$
    C) $(1, -3)$
    D) $(-1, -3)$

$$y = 2x - 3$$

6. In the equation above, if $y = 17$, what is the value of x ?

7. What value of x satisfies the equation $6(x - 2) = 3(x + 3)$?

8. If $7(2a + b) - 1 = 27$, then $2a + b =$

LEVEL 1: PASSPORT TO ADVANCED MATH

9. Which of the following expressions is equivalent to $3a + 6b + 9c$?

    A) $3(a + 2b + 3c)$
    B) $3(a + 2b + 15c)$
    C) $3(a + 10b + 15c)$
    D) $3(a + 2b) + 3c$

10. Which of the following is equivalent to the sum of $3 - x + x^2$ and $2x - x^2$?

    A) $2x^2 + 3$
    B) $x + 3$
    C) $3x$
    D) $2x^2 - 3x + 3$

11. Which of the following is equivalent to $\left(\frac{x^3}{x^2}\right)^5$?

    A) x^5
    B) x^{10}
    C) x^{20}
    D) x^{25}

12. If $4x^2 - 12x = 40$, what are the possible values for x ?

    A) -2 and 5
    B) -5 and 2
    C) -5 and -8
    D) -5 and -16

x	$p(x)$	$q(x)$	$r(x)$
1	1	2	3
2	2	5	-3
3	5	2	-3
4	-2	4	-2

13. The table above gives some values of the functions p, q, and r. At which value x does $q(x) = p(x) + r(x)$?

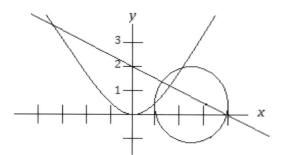

14. The graphs of three equations in two unknowns are shown in the xy-plane above. How many solutions does the system of equations have?

15. If $\frac{20}{x^2+1} = 5$, what is the value of $x^2 + 1$?

16. If $5t^2 - 35 = 13 - 3t^2$, what is the value of $7t^2$?

LEVEL 1: PROBLEM SOLVING

Questions 17 - 19 refer to the following information.

A census was given to determine information about the number of children from households in a small community. 100 families were surveyed and the results are shown in the table below.

Number of Children Per Household

Number of Children	0	1	2	3	More than 3
Households with that number of children	11	21	35	17	16

17. How many households that were part of the census data have exactly 4 children?

    A) 2
    B) 8
    C) 16
    D) Cannot be determined from the given information

18. What percent of the households that were surveyed have at least 3 children?

    A) 8%
    B) 16%
    C) 17%
    D) 33%

19. If a household is chosen at random, what is the probability that the household will have 2 children?

    A) 0.175
    B) 0.35
    C) 0.7
    D) Cannot be determined from the given information

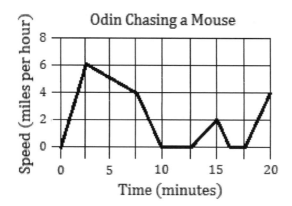

20. Odin the cat chased a mouse for twenty minutes. His time and speed are displayed in the graph above. According to the graph, which of the following is the best estimate for the number of minutes that Odin was not moving during the chase.

   A) 0
   B) 1
   C) 2
   D) 4

21. A box containing 20 ribbons includes 3 red ribbons, 5 blue ribbons, and 12 yellow ribbons. What percent of the ribbons in the box are yellow?

   A) 20%
   B) 40%
   C) 60%
   D) 80%

22. A merchant issued rebates totaling $200 to its customers. Some customers received a $15 rebate and other customers received a $20 rebate. If at least one customer received $15 and at least one customer received $20, what is one possible number of $20 rebates?

23. A company sells advertising for their magazine in blocks of 6 lines of text. If the company places 18 lines of advertising text per page, with 7 pages of advertising per magazine, and 12 issues of the magazine are released each year, what is the total number of six-line advertisements the company can sell in one year?

24. What is the range of the following 9 test grades?

$$89, 66, 75, 91, 56, 92, 76, 71, 76$$

LEVEL 1: GEOMETRY AND COMPLEX NUMBERS

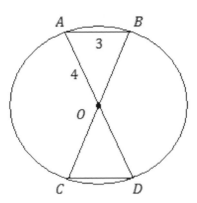

25. In the figure above, if O is the center of the circle, and $\overline{AD}$ and $\overline{BC}$ are diameters, which of the following statements is true?

   A) $OC > 4$
   B) $CD > 3$
   C) $CD = 3$
   D) $OD = 3$

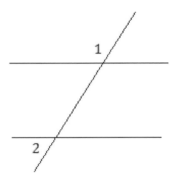

26. The figure above shows two parallel lines cut by a transversal. Which of the following statements regarding angles 1 and 2 is true?

   A) $m\angle 1 = m\angle 2$
   B) $m\angle 1 = 90° - m\angle 2$
   C) $m\angle 1 = 180° - m\angle 2$
   D) $m\angle 1 = 360° - m\angle 2$

27. For $i = \sqrt{-1}$, the sum $(8 - 7i) + (2 + 3i)$ is equal to

   A) $10 - 4i$
   B) $10 + 4i$
   C) $6 - 4i$
   D) $6 + 4i$

$10 - 4i$

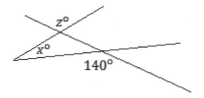

28. In the figure above, $x = 25$. What is the value of z ?

29. If the degree measures of the three angles of a triangle are $k°$, $k°$, and $81°$, what is the value of k?

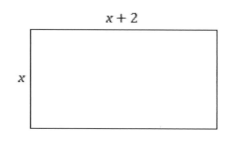

30. If the area of the rectangle above is 15, what is the value of x ?

31. The interior dimensions of a rectangular box are 3 inches by 8 inches by 6 inches. What is the volume, in cubic inches, of the interior of the box?

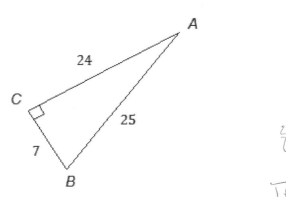

32. In the figure above, what is $\sin A$?

LEVEL 2: HEART OF ALGEBRA

$$19 - \frac{3}{14}x = 7 + \frac{6}{7}x$$

33. What is the value of x in the equation above?

    A) $\frac{14}{5}$

    B) 7

    C) $\frac{56}{5}$

    D) 14

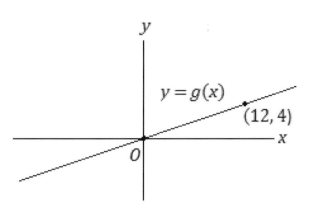

34. In the xy-plane above, a point (not shown) with coordinates (a, b) lies on the graph of the linear function g. If a and b are positive integers, what is the ratio of b to a ?

    A) 3 to 1
    B) 1 to 3
    C) 2 to 1
    D) 1 to 2

35. The graph of which of the following equations is a line that is parallel to the line with equation $y = -2x - 3$?

    A) $2x - y = 1$
    B) $y - 2x = 1$
    C) $4x + 2y = 1$
    D) $2x - 4y = 1$

36. A pipe is used to fill a swimming pool with water. The amount of water in the pool is given by the equation $V = 12t + 200$, where t is the number of minutes since the pipe began filling the pool and V is the volume, in gallons, of water in the pool. In the equation, what are the meanings of the numbers 12 and 200 ?

    A) The number 12 is the rate of increase, in gallons per minute, in the volume of the water in the pool, and the number 200 is the initial number of gallons of water in the pool.
    B) The number 12 is the rate of decrease, in gallons per minute, in the volume of the water in the pool, and the number 200 is the initial number of gallons of water in the pool.
    C) The number 12 is the rate of decrease, in gallons per minute, in the volume of the water in the pool, and the pool holds 200 gallons of water.
    D) The number 12 is the number of minutes it will take to fill the pool, and the pool holds 200 gallons of water.

$$\frac{1}{3}x = 9$$
$$y - \frac{1}{3}x = 2$$

37. The system of equations above has solution (x, y). What is the value of y ?

    A) $\frac{9}{2}$
    B) $\frac{11}{2}$
    C) 7
    D) 11

38. A toy manufacturer uses the function $P(x) = 12x - 1500$ to estimate their profit $P(x)$, in dollars, when they produce x toys. Based on this model, how many toys should the manufacturer produce to realize a profit of \$5136 ?

39. * What is the slope of the line passing through the points $(-\frac{1}{2}, -3)$ and $(2, -\frac{1}{3})$?

40. If $7x - 2y = 22$, what is the value of $\frac{3}{11}(7x - 2y)$?

LEVEL 2: PASSPORT TO ADVANCED MATH

$$100x^2 - 64y^2 = (ax + by)(ax - by)$$

41. In the equation above, a and b are constants. Which of the following could be the value of $\frac{b}{a}$?

    A) $\frac{4}{5}$
    B) $\frac{16}{25}$
    C) $\frac{3}{5}$
    D) $\frac{8}{25}$

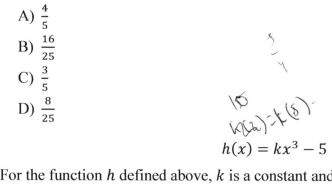

$$h(x) = kx^3 - 5$$

42. For the function h defined above, k is a constant and $h(2) = 5$. What is the value of $h(-2)$?

    A) -15
    B) 0
    C) 5
    D) 19

$$(2x^2 + x - 5) - (-2x^2 - 2x + 1)$$

43. Which of the following expressions is equivalent to the one above?

    A) $3x - 6$
    B) $-x - 4$
    C) $4x^2 + 3x - 6$
    D) $4x^2 - x - 4$

    $4x^2 + 3x - 6$

44. If $2^{3y} = 64$, what is the value of y ?

    A) 3
    B) 2
    C) 1
    D) 0

45. If $c = 3\sqrt{3b}$, what is $3b$ in terms of c ?

    A) $\frac{c}{3}$
    B) $\frac{c^2}{3}$
    C) $\frac{c^2}{9}$
    D) $9c^2$

    $\left(\dfrac{c}{3}\right)^2$

$$3y = -\frac{x}{2}$$
$$3y^2 - 2y + 1 = x$$

46. Which of the following ordered pairs (x, y) satisfies both of the above equations?

    A) $(17, -2)$
    B) $(-12, 2)$
    C) $(2, 1)$
    D) $(6, -1)$

47. If $x > 0$, what is one possible solution to the equation $x^5(x^4 - 7) = -6x^3$?

$$\sqrt{c - 10} + x^2 = 50 + x$$

48. In the equation above, c is a constant. If $x = 7$, what is the value of c ?

    8

    64

LEVEL 2: PROBLEM SOLVING

49. During a renovation project, a city's main highway was extended from 85 miles to 88 miles. Of the following, which is closest to the increase in the highway's length, in kilometers? (1 mile is approximately 1.6 kilometers)

    A) 4.5
    B) 4.7
    C) 5.1
    D) 5.4

Questions 50 - 52 refer to the following information.

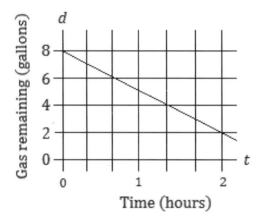

Kenneth is driving from his home to a conference. The graph above displays the amount of gas g, in gallons, remaining in Kenneth's car t minutes after he begins driving.

50. Which of the following represents the relationship between t and g ?

    A) $g = -3t$
    B) $g = -3t + 8$
    C) $g = -\frac{1}{3}t$
    D) $g = -\frac{1}{3}t - 8$

51. What does the g-intercept represent in the graph?

    A) The total amount of gas used during the trip
    B) The total number of hours the trip took
    C) The initial amount of gas in the car's gas tank
    D) The decrease in the amount of gas remaining in the car per hour of driving

52. If Kenneth does not fill his car's gas tank during the trip, when will he run out of gas?

    A) 2 hours after he begins his trip.
    B) 2 and a half hours after he begins his trip
    C) 160 minutes after he begins his trip
    D) 200 minutes after he begins his trip

53. The scatterplot below shows the relationship between the mean monthly heating cost, in dollars, and the mean monthly temperature, in degrees Fahrenheit (°F), in 20 houses in a small town. The line of best fit is also shown.

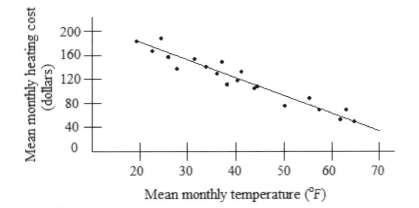

Based on the line of best fit, which of the following is closest to the predicted mean heating cost, in dollars, for a month when the mean temperature is 55°F ?

A) $40
B) $80
C) $120
D) $160

54. * A geologist estimates that a glacier is moving at the rate of 17 feet per year. According to this estimate, how long will it take, in years, for this glacier to move 24.5 yards? (1 yard = 3 feet)

55. A child likes to collect stuffed animals. The ratio of the number of stuffed pigs he has collected to the number of stuffed cows he has collected is 3 to 1. If the child has 6 stuffed pigs, how many stuffed cows does he have?

56. Jeff has taken 6 of 10 equally weighted math tests this semester, and he has an average score of exactly 82 points. How many points does he need to earn on the 7th test to bring his average score up to exactly 83 points?

LEVEL 2: GEOMETRY AND COMPLEX NUMBERS

57. In $\triangle CAT$, $\angle A$ is a right angle. Which of the following is equal to $\tan T$?

A) $\frac{CA}{CT}$

B) $\frac{CA}{AT}$

C) $\frac{CT}{CA}$

D) $\frac{CT}{AT}$

58. In the xy-plane, the point $(0,3)$ is the center of a circle that has radius 3. Which of the following is NOT a point on the circle?

    A) $(0,6)$
    B) $(-3,6)$
    C) $(3,3)$
    D) $(-3,3)$

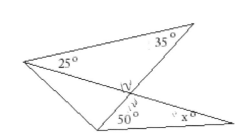

59. In the figure above, what is the value of x ?

60. * The measure of angle X is $12°$ less than the measure of angle Y. To the nearest tenth of a radian, how much less is the measure of angle X than the measure of angle Y ?

61. The volume of a pyramid is $10,000$ cubic feet. If the length, width, and height of the pyramid are in the ratio $2:3:5$, what is the area of the base of the pyramid, in square feet?

62. Each angle of triangle CAT is congruent to one of the angles of triangle DOG. If $DO = 5$, $DG = 6$, $OG = 7$, $CA = 21$, and $\angle T$ has the largest measure of all angles in triangle CAT, what is the perimeter of triangle CAT ?

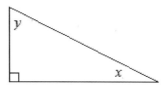

63. In the triangle above, the sine of $y°$ is 0.8. What is the cosine of $x°$?

64. What is the value of the expression $i^3 - i^2 + i$? $(i = \sqrt{-1})$

LEVEL 3: HEART OF ALGEBRA

65. A grocery store sells candy bars individually and in packs of 12. During a certain week, the grocery store sold a total of 315 candy bars, of which 51 were sold individually. Which expression gives the number of packs of candy bars sold during that week?

    A) $\frac{315}{12} + 51$
    B) $\frac{315}{12} - 51$
    C) $\frac{315+51}{12}$
    D) $\frac{315-51}{12}$

66. In the xy-plane, line k has a slope of $\frac{5}{7}$ and passes through the point $(0,5)$. What is the x-intercept of line k ?

    A) -8
    B) -7
    C) 1
    D) 5

Questions 67 - 70 refer to the following information.

$$C(x) = 2600 + 0.7x$$
$$R(x) = 3x$$
$$P(x) = R(x) - C(x)$$

The manager of a convenience store is submitting a report to the store's owner, estimating the monthly costs, C, monthly revenue, R, and monthly profit, P, in dollars. The functions above express each of these three quantities in terms of the number of customers, x, that make purchases in a given month. The monthly costs, C, consist of fixed costs for rent, utilities, and payroll, and a variable cost for inventory based upon the number of customers in the given month.

67. What is the best interpretation of the number 2600 in the definition of $C(x)$?

    A) The cost for the convenience store to acquire enough customers to break even
    B) The average cost that the convenience store spends per month on expenses
    C) The cost for a month of inventory
    D) The cost for a month of rent, utilities, and payroll

68. What is the best interpretation of the number 3 in the definition of $R(x)$?

    A) On average, each customer at the convenience store buys 3 items.
    B) On average, each customer at the convenience store spends \$3.
    C) On average, it costs the convenience store \$3 to acquire a customer.
    D) On average, each item at the convenience store costs \$3.

69. * The manager estimates that the profit for the month of January will be between \$620 and \$850. Which of the following inequalities gives the best estimate for the number of customers, x, that will make a purchase at the convenience store in January?

    A) $1200 \le x \le 1300$
    B) $1300 \le x \le 1400$
    C) $1400 \le x \le 1500$
    D) $1500 \le x \le 1600$

70. * Assuming that for the month of February the equations given in the manager's report are accurate, what is the least number of customers that need to make a purchase at the store in February in order for the store to at least break even that month?

    A) 1130
    B) 1131
    C) 1132
    D) 1133

$$\frac{1}{3}(3x + 2y) = \frac{7}{3}$$
$$x = 4y$$

71. The system of equations above has solution (x, y). What is the value of y ?

72. At a pet store, each frog is priced at \$1 and each salamander is priced at \$8. Jeff purchased 14 amphibians at the store for a total price of \$42. How many frogs did Jeff purchase?

LEVEL 3: PASSPORT TO ADVANCED MATH

73. The polynomial $z^4 + 6z^3 + 5z^2 - 24z - 36$ can be written as $(z^2 - 4)(z + 3)^2$. What are all the roots of the polynomial?

    A) -3 and 2
    B) -3, 2, and 4
    C) -3, -2, and 2
    D) -2, 2, and 3

74. Which of the following expressions is equivalent to $(9b^2)^{\frac{1}{2}}$?

    A) $9b$
    B) $\sqrt{\frac{9b}{2}}$
    C) $\frac{9}{2}|b|$
    D) $3|b|$

$$3ax^2 + 6bx + 9c + 5 = 17$$

75. Based on the equation above, what is the value of $ax^2 + 2bx + 3c$?

    A) 3
    B) 4
    C) 12
    D) 24

76. The formula $E = \frac{1}{2}mv^2$ gives the kinetic energy of an object with mass m that is moving with speed v. Based on this formula, express m in terms of E and v.

    A) $m = 2Ev^2$

    B) $m = \frac{2E}{v^2}$

    C) $m = 2E\sqrt{v}$

    D) $m = \frac{2E}{\sqrt{v}}$

$$x(2x - 3) = 5$$

77. Which of the following lists all solutions to the quadratic equation above?

    A) $0, \frac{3}{2}$

    B) $0, -\frac{3}{2}$

    C) $-1, \frac{5}{2}$

    D) $-\frac{5}{2}, 1$

78. If the equation $y = (x - 5)(x + 7)$ is graphed in the xy-plane, what is the x-coordinate of the parabola's vertex?

    A) -5
    B) -1
    C) 1
    D) 5

79. If $b = 5a^3 - 2a + 7$, $c = 2a^2 + a + 3$, and $3c - b = da^3 + ea^2 + fa + g$, what is the value of $d + e + f + g$?

$$x^2 + 5x = 14$$

80. In the quadratic equation above, find the positive solution for x.

LEVEL 3: PROBLEM SOLVING

Questions 81 - 82 refer to the following information.

The amount of revenue that a grocery store takes in each month is directly proportional to the number of people that enter the store that month. In January, the grocery store took $2800 in total revenue and 350 people entered the store.

81. * In February, 400 people entered the grocery store. How much revenue did the grocery store make? (Disregard the dollar sign when gridding in your answer.)

137

82. * The owner of the grocery store donates 12% of the revenue each month to a charity and uses 27% for marketing and other expenses. The rest of the money earned is the retailer's profit. What is the profit in a month where 400 people enter the grocery store? (Disregard the dollar sign when gridding in your answer.)

Questions 83 – 84 refer to the following information.

Fabric	Cost per square foot in US dollars	Cost per square foot in British pounds
Cotton	0.41	0.31
Wool	0.66	0.50
Silk	1.17	0.89

The table above gives the typical cost per square foot of several fabrics in both US dollars and British pounds on November 1, 2017.

83. * If d dollars is equivalent to p pounds on November 1, 2017, which of the following best represents the relationship between d and p ?

A) $p = 0.76d$

B) $p = 1.32d$

C) $pd = 0.76$

D) $pd = 1.32$

84. * If a tapestry using \$41 of material is made entirely from c square feet of cotton, w square feet of wool, and s square feet of silk fabric, which of the following expresses c in terms of w and s ?

A) $c = 100 - \frac{1}{0.41}(0.66w + 1.17s)$

B) $c = 100 - \frac{1}{0.41}(0.66w - 1.17s)$

C) $c = 100 + \frac{1}{0.41}(0.66w + 1.17s)$

D) $c = 100 + \frac{1}{0.41}(0.66w - 1.17s)$

Type of Professor	Favorite activity		Total
	Research	Teaching	
Mathematics	521	326	847
Physics	226	371	597
Total	747	697	1444

85. * On a survey, 847 math professors and 597 physics professors specified whether they preferred teaching or research. The table above summarizes these results. If one of the professors is chosen at random, which of the following is closest to the probability that the chosen professor is a physics professor that prefers teaching?

    A) 0.26
    B) 0.53
    C) 0.62
    D) 0.89

86. * A survey was conducted among a randomly chosen sample of 250 single men and 250 single women about whether they owned any guinea pigs or rabbits. The table below displays a summary of the survey results.

	Guinea Pigs Only	Rabbits Only	Both	Neither	Total
Men	92	14	18	126	250
Women	75	42	35	98	250
Total	167	56	53	224	500

What fraction of the people surveyed who said they own both guinea pigs and rabbits are women? Round your answer to the nearest tenth.

87. * A cheetah is running at a speed of 70 miles per hour. What is the cheetah's speed, to the nearest whole number, in meters per minute? (1 mile = 1609.34 meters)

88. The mean score of 10 people playing a video game is 1436 points. If the lowest individual score is removed, the mean score of the remaining 9 people is 1400 points. What is the lowest score?

LEVEL 3: GEOMETRY AND COMPLEX NUMBERS

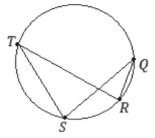

89. In the figure above, angles TSQ and TRQ are inscribed in the circle. Which of the following statements is true?

   A) $m\angle TSQ = m\angle TRQ$
   B) $m\angle TSQ > m\angle TRQ$
   C) $m\angle TSQ < m\angle TRQ$
   D) Not enough information is given to determine a relationship between $\angle TSQ$ and $\angle TRQ$.

Questions 90 - 92 refer to the following information.

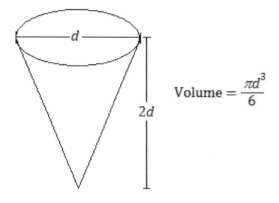

The cone above can hold a maximum volume of 8 fluid ounces (approximately 14.5 cubic inches).

90. How many times can the cone be filled by a jug containing $\frac{1}{2}$ gallon of liquid? (1 gallon = 128 fluid ounces)

   A) 4
   B) 8
   C) 16
   D) 32

91. * Which of the following is closest to the value of d, in inches?

   A) 2
   B) 3
   C) 4
   D) 5

92. A liquid is poured into the cone at a constant rate. Which of the following graphs best illustrates the height of the liquid in the cone as it is being filled?

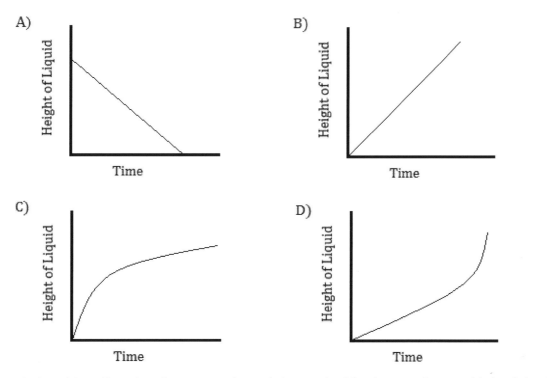

93. A circle with radius 5 and center at $(-3, 7)$ is graphed in the xy-plane. Which of the following could be an equation of the circle?

    A) $(x + 3)^2 - (y - 7)^2 = 5$
    B) $(x + 3)^2 - (y - 7)^2 = 25$
    C) $(x + 3)^2 + (y - 7)^2 = 5$
    D) $(x + 3)^2 + (y - 7)^2 = 25$

Note: Figure not drawn to scale.

94. In the triangle above, y is an integer. If $39 < x < 40$, what is one possible value of y?

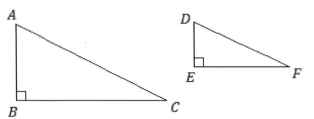

95. In the figure above, the two triangles are similar, with vertices A, B, and C corresponding to vertices D, E, and F, respectively. If $\tan A = 2.36$, what is the value of $\tan D$?

96. The complex number expression $i^2 + i^4 + i^5 + i^8 + i^9$ can be rewritten in the form $a + bi$, where a and b are real numbers, and $i = \sqrt{-1}$. What is the value of $a + b$?

LEVEL 4: HEART OF ALGEBRA

97. A high school has a $1000 budget to buy calculators. Each scientific calculator will cost the school $12.97 and each graphing calculator will cost the school $73.89. Which of the following inequalities represents the possible number of scientific calculators S and graphing calculators G that the school can purchase while staying within their specified budget?

    A) $12.97S + 73.89G > 1000$

    B) $12.97S + 73.89G \leq 1000$

    C) $\frac{12.97}{S} + \frac{73.89}{G} > 1000$

    D) $\frac{12.97}{S} + \frac{73.89}{G} \leq 1000$

98. In the xy-plane, which of the following does NOT contain any points that are part of the solution set to $5x + 2y > 10$?

    A) The y-axis
    B) The region where x and y are both positive
    C) The region where x and y are both negative
    D) The region where x is negative and y is positive

$$T = 25 + 3c$$

99. The equation above is used to model the number of chirps, c, made by a certain species of cricket in one minute, and the temperature, T, in degrees Fahrenheit. According to this model, what is the meaning of the number 3 in the equation?

    A) If a cricket chirps three more times in one minute, then the temperature, in Fahrenheit, will be one degree higher.

    B) If a cricket chirps three fewer times in one minute, then the temperature, in Fahrenheit, will be one degree higher.

    C) If a cricket chirps one more time in one minute, then the temperature, in Fahrenheit, will be three degrees higher.

    D) If a cricket chirps one fewer time in one minute, then the temperature, in Fahrenheit, will be three degrees higher.

$$5x - 3y = 7$$
$$-30x + by = 9$$

100. In the system of equations above, b is a constant and x and y are variables. If the system has no solutions, what is the value of b ?

    A) -6
    B) 5
    C) 18
    D) There is no such value of b.

101. The graph of a line in the xy-plane crosses the x-axis at the point $(3, 0)$ and the y-axis at the point $(0, -4)$. The line passes through the point $(9, a)$ for what value of a ?

102. A limousine service charges a fixed amount for up to an hour of limousine service plus an amount for each person being transported. A limousine transporting 4 people within an hour costs \$160 and a limousine transporting 7 people within an hour costs \$210. How many people are being transported by the limousine if the charge is \$260, assuming that the limousine service will be used for at most an hour?

$$4x = 5 - 3y$$
$$3y - 2x = 2$$

103. If (x, y) is a solution to the above system of equations, what is the value of $x + y$?

104. While playing a certain game, players obtain blue cards and red cards. At the end of the game, each player's score is obtained by subtracting twice the number of red cards from three times the number of blue cards. A player with a final score of 27 is holding 29 cards at the end of the game. How many blue cards is the player holding?

LEVEL 4: PASSPORT TO ADVANCED MATH

$$5(x - 1)(2x + 3)$$

105. Which of the following expressions is equivalent to the one above?

    A) $30x^2$
    B) $5x^2 - 15$
    C) $10x^2 - 15$
    D) $10x^2 + 5x - 15$

106. If $y = x^{-\frac{2}{3}}$, where $x > 0$, what is x in terms of y ?

    A) $\dfrac{1}{\sqrt{y^3}}$

    B) $\dfrac{1}{\sqrt[3]{y^2}}$

    C) $-\sqrt{y^3}$

    D) $-\sqrt[3]{y^2}$

$$\frac{x}{2} = \frac{3x + 19}{7}$$

107. In the equation above, $3x + 19$ could be equal to which of the following?

    A) -133
    B) -19
    C) 38
    D) 133

108. Which of the following is a value of x for which the expression $-\frac{11}{x^2 + 3x - 10}$ is undefined?

    A) -5
    B) -2
    C) 1
    D) 5

$$x - 3y^2 + 6y + 2 = 0$$

109. The equation above represents a parabola in the xy-plane. Which of the following equivalent forms of the equation displays the x-intercept(s) of the parabola as constants or coefficients?

    A) $x = 3(y - 1)^2 - 5$
    B) $x + 5 = 3(y - 1)^2$
    C) $x = 3y^2 - 6y - 2$
    D) $y = 1 \pm \sqrt{\frac{x+5}{3}}$

110. The function g is defined by $g(x) = (x + 3)^3(x + 5)$. If $g(k - 4.7) = 0$, what is one possible value of k?

111. In the xy-plane, the graph of $y = (x + 3)^2 - 2$ is the image of the graph of $y = (x + 7)^2 + 1$ after a translation of a units to the right and b units down. What is the value of ab?

$$2x^2 - x - 3 = 0$$

112. If c is a positive solution to the equation above, what is the value of c?

LEVEL 4: PROBLEM SOLVING

113. A block is sliding down a ramp that drops 3 centimeters in elevation for every 5 centimeters along the length of the ramp. The top of the ramp, where the back edge of the block is initially placed, is at 60 centimeters elevation, and the block is sliding at 10 centimeters per second down the ramp. What is the elevation of the ramp, in centimeters, at the point where the back of the block passes t seconds after being released?

   A) $60 - \frac{3}{5}t$

   B) $60 - 3t$

   C) $60 - 6t$

   D) $60 - 9t$

Questions 114 - 115 refer to the following information.

Boat	Price in dollars	Average monthly fuel cost in dollars
Boat 1	50,000	230
Boat 2	200,000	1010
Boat 3	180,000	906
Boat 4	375,000	1920

During his lifetime, Daniel purchased four different boats. The table above shows the purchase price, in dollars, for the four different boats and the average monthly fuel cost that Daniel paid for each boat, in dollars.

114. The relationship between the average monthly fuel cost f, in dollars, and the purchase price x, in thousands of dollars, can be modeled by a linear function. Which of the following linear functions best represents the relationship?

   A) $f(x) = 2.2x + 120$
   B) $f(x) = 3.7x + 45$
   C) $f(x) = 5.2x - 30$
   D) $f(x) = 6.1x - 75$

115. * When Daniel bought Boat 3, he received a 30% discount off the original price, and an additional 10% off the discounted price for paying the full amount at the time of purchase. Which of the following is the best estimate for the original price, in dollars, of Boat 3 ?

   A) 185,000
   B) 286,000
   C) 322,000
   D) 450,000

116. A phone manufacturer hires a tester to determine the average lifespan of their current phone model. The tester selects 200 phones at random from the phones produced that day and finds that the life of the phone has a mean of 400 days with an associated margin of error of 72 days. Which of the following is the most appropriate conclusion based on these data?

   A) It is plausible that the mean life of all phones ever produced by the manufacturer is between 328 and 472 days.
   B) It is plausible that the mean life of all phones produced by the manufacturer that day is between 328 and 472 days.
   C) All phones ever produced by the manufacturer have a life between 328 and 472 days.
   D) All phones produced by the manufacturer that day have a life between 328 and 472 days.

117. Which scatterplot shows a relationship that is appropriately modeled with the equation $y = ax^b$ where $a > 0$ and $b < 0$?

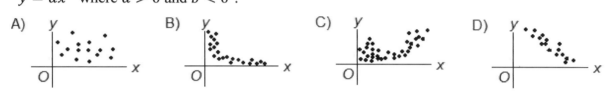

118. The average (arithmetic mean) salary of employees at an advertising firm with P employees, in thousands of dollars, is 53, and the average salary of employees at an advertising firm with Q employees, in thousands of dollars, is 95. When the salaries of both firms are combined, the average salary in thousands of dollars is 83. What is the value of $\frac{P}{Q}$?

119. * Jessica has two cats named Mittens and Fluffy. Last year Mittens weighed 12 pounds, and Fluffy weighed 19 pounds. Fluffy was placed on a diet, and his weight decreased by 20%. Mittens weight has increased by 20%. By what percentage did Mitten's and Fluffy's combined weight decrease, to the nearest tenth of a percent?

	At least 6 feet tall	Less than 6 feet tall
Male		
Female		
Total	15	34

120. * The incomplete table above classifies the number of students by height for the twelfth-grade students at Washington High School. There are twice as many male students that are less than 6 feet tall as there are male students that are at least 6 feet tall, and there are four times as many female students that are less than 6 feet tall as there are female students that are at least 6 feet tall. What is the probability that a randomly selected student that is at least 6 feet tall is female?

146

LEVEL 4: GEOMETRY AND COMPLEX NUMBERS

121. If n is an integer greater than 35, how many different triangles are there with sides of length 19, 21, and x ?

    A) One
    B) Two
    C) Three
    D) Four

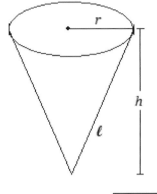

$$SA = \pi r^2 + \pi r \sqrt{r^2 + h^2}$$

122. The formula above can be used to calculate the total surface area of the right circular cone shown, where h is the height of the cone, and r is the radius of the circular base. What must the expression $\sqrt{r^2 + h^2}$ represent?

    A) The circumferences of the circular base
    B) The area of the circular base
    C) The lateral surface area of the cone
    D) The length of line segment ℓ

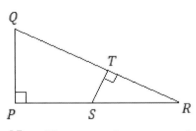

Note: Figure not drawn to scale.

123. In the right triangle PQR above, $SR = 9$, and $QR = 24$. If the length of $\overline{PR}$ is 2 units less than three times the length of $\overline{TR}$, what is the length of $\overline{PR}$?

    A) $\dfrac{16}{21}$
    B) $\dfrac{30}{7}$
    C) 6
    D) 16

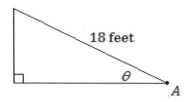

124.* In the figure above a person is standing at point A, and his feet are at a distance of 18 feet from the top of a tree. The angle of elevation, θ, from point A to the top of the tree is 20°. Given that the sine of 70° is approximately 0.94, which of the following is closest to the distance from the person to the base of the tree?

    A) 14 feet
    B) 15 feet
    C) 16 feet
    D) 17 feet

125. Suppose that $0 < k < 90$, $0 < t < 90$, and $\cos k° = \sin t°$. If $k = \frac{1}{3}z - 42$ and $t = \frac{2}{3}z + 12$, what is the value of z ?

126. A rectangle has a perimeter of 22 meters and an area of 28 square meters. What is the shortest of the side lengths, in meters, of the rectangle?

127. In the (x, y) coordinate plane, what is the radius of the circle having the points $(2, -4)$ and $(-4, 4)$ as endpoints of a diameter?

$$\frac{2i - 3}{5i - 1}$$

128. If the expression above is written in the form $a + bi$, where a and b are real numbers, and $i = \sqrt{-1}$, what is the value of a ?

LEVEL 5: HEART OF ALGEBRA

129. Jeff wants to save enough money to purchase and maintain a grand piano. The piano costs $10,000 and maintenance and tuning costs average $40 per month. Jeff has already saved $7,000 and he plans to save an additional $420 per month. Which of the following inequalities can be used to determine the number of months, t, Jeff needs to save in order to have enough money to buy the piano and pay for 12 months of maintenance and tuning?

    A) $10{,}000 - 40 \cdot 12 \le 7{,}000 - 420t$
    B) $10{,}000 + 40 \cdot 12 \le 7{,}000 + 420t$
    C) $10{,}000 - 40t \le 7{,}000 - 320 \cdot 12$
    D) $10{,}000 + 40t \le 7{,}000 + 320 \cdot 12$

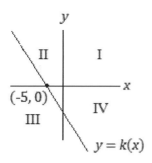

130. The graph of the function $k(x)$ is shown in the xy-plane above. If $h(x) = \frac{1}{3}x + \frac{3}{2}$, in which quadrant does the graph of $y = h(x)$ intersect the graph of $y = k(x)$?

    A) I
    B) II
    C) III
    D) IV

131. An alligator ran at a rate of 8 miles per hour and then swam at a rate of 15 miles per hour. The alligator travelled no less than 5 miles in no more than a half hour. Which of the following systems of inequalities represents the situation, given that r is the number of miles the alligator ran and s is the number of miles the alligator swam?

    A) $r + s \geq 5$
        $8r + 15s \geq 0.5$

    B) $r + s \leq 0.5$
        $8r + 15s \leq 5$

    C) $r + s \geq 5$
        $\frac{r}{8} + \frac{s}{15} \leq 0.5$

    D) $r + s \leq 5$
        $\frac{r}{8} + \frac{s}{15} \geq 0.5$

132. Gary takes a New York City cab 6 miles to work and must pay \$17.50 for the cab ride. After work, Gary takes another New York City cab 10 miles to visit his family and must pay \$27.50. During both of these rides, Gary was charged a "drop fee" (an initial charge when the cab's meter was activated) of d dollars, plus an additional m dollars for each $\frac{1}{5}$ of a mile travelled. What is the value of md ?

Questions 133 - 134 refer to the following information.

The quantity of a product supplied (called the *supply*) and the quantity of the product demanded (called the *demand*) in an economic market are functions of the price of the product. The market is said to be in *equilibrium* when the supply and demand are equal. The price at equilibrium is called the *equilibrium price*, and the quantity at equilibrium is called the *equilibrium demand*. Consider the following supply and demand functions, where p is the price, in dollars, s is the supply function, and d is the demand function.

$$s = \frac{2}{3}p + 15$$

$$d = -\frac{1}{3}p + 99$$

133. What is the equilibrium price? (Disregard the dollar sign when gridding your answer.)

134. What is the equilibrium demand?

$$x + y = \frac{16k}{5}$$

$$\frac{1}{3}x = k$$

135. In the system of equations above, k is a constant such that $0 < k < \frac{1}{5}$. Given that (x, y) is a solution to the system of equations, what is one possible value of y ?

$$-\frac{7}{5}jx - \frac{14}{15} = 3x + k$$

136. In the equation above, j and k are constants. If the equation has infinitely many solutions, what is the value of jk ?

LEVEL 5: PASSPORT TO ADVANCED MATH

137. If $x + y = 2k - 1$, and $x^2 + y^2 = 9 - 4k + 2k^2$, what is xy in terms of k ?

    A) $k - 2$
    B) $(k - 2)^2$
    C) $(k + 2)^2$
    D) $k^2 - 4$

$$(x^4 y^5)^{\frac{1}{4}}(x^8 y^5)^{\frac{1}{5}} = x^{\frac{j}{5}} y^{\frac{k}{4}}$$

138. In the equation above, j and k are constants. If the equation is true for all positive real values of x and y, what is the value of $j - k$?

    A) 3
    B) 4
    C) 5
    D) 6

139. Let x, y, and z be numbers such that $-x < y < z < x$. Which of the following must be true?

    I. $z - y > 0$
   II. $y + z > 0$
  III. $|y| < x$

    A) I only
    B) III only
    C) I and III only
    D) I, II, and III

$$q(x) = (x - 3)(x + 5)$$

140. Which of the following is an equivalent form of the function q above in which the minimum value of q appears as a constant or coefficient?

    A) $q(x) = x^2 - 15$
    B) $q(x) = x^2 + 2x - 15$
    C) $q(x) = (x + 1)^2 - 16$
    D) $q(x) = (x - 1)^2 - 16$

$$x^3 + 2x^2 + 5x + 10 = 0$$

141. The equation above has one real solution, a, and two complex solutions $\pm bi$. What is the value of b^2 ?

$$x^2 + 2x - 1$$
$$2x^2 - x + 3$$

142. The product of the two polynomials shown above can be written in the form $ax^4 + bx^3 + cx^2 + dx + e$. What is the value of $\frac{b}{d}$?

$$\frac{x^2 + 7x - 60}{x - 5}$$

143. The expression above is equivalent to $x + a$, where $x \neq 5$. What is the value of a ?

144. An architect wants to design a bathroom with a rectangular area of 272 square feet. He also wants the width of the bathroom to be 1 foot longer than the length. What will be the width of the bathroom, in feet?

LEVEL 5: PROBLEM SOLVING

Questions 145 - 146 refer to the following information.

743 children from the United States, aged 6 through 11, were tested to see if they were overweight. The data are shown in the table below.

	Overweight	Not overweight	Total
Ages 6-8	31	286	317
Ages 9-11	163	263	426
Total	194	549	743

145. In 2014, the total population of children between 6 and 11 years old, inclusive, in the United States was about 74.3 million. If the test results are used to estimate information about children across the country, which of the following is the best estimate of the total number of children between 9 and 11 years old in the United States who were overweight in 2014 ?

    A) 3,100,000
    B) 16,300,000
    C) 19,400,000
    D) 42,600,000

146. * According to the table, which of the following statements is most likely to be true about children between 6 and 11 years old, inclusive, in the United States?

    A) The probability that a 6-8 year old is overweight is greater than the probability that an overweight child aged 6-11 is less than 9 years old.
    B) The probability that a 6-11 year old is overweight is greater than the probability that a 9-11 year old is not overweight.
    C) The probability that an overweight 6-11 year old is at least 9 years old is greater than the probability that a 6-11 year old is not overweight.
    D) The probability that a 6-8 year old is overweight is greater than the probability that a 9-11 year old is not overweight.

147. A nutritionist wants to determine whether a certain diet improves the performance of members of competitive teams in a certain town. To test the diet, the nutritionist arranges for all the female swim team members from the town to stay on the diet for three months. The nutritionist then compares the performance of these swimmers to swim team members from previous years. Which of the following would NOT improve the quality of the study?

    A) Including members of all the girl's competitive teams from the town in the study
    B) Including women who are not members of competitive teams in the study
    C) Including male swim team members in the study
    D) Randomly assigning half the female swim team members to use the new diet while the other half continues to eat as they would normally

Questions 148 -149 refer to the following information.

A diplomat is researching the relationship between the price of a certain export coming from a specific country and the number of adversaries that country has. The diplomat defines an adversary to be a nation that purchases the export, but will not do business with that specific country. 20 countries are chosen at random, and for each of these countries, the diplomat records the number of its adversaries and its price for the export. The results are shown in the scatterplot below and the line of best fit is drawn.

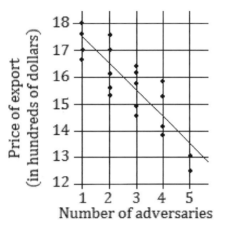

148. The line of best fit passes through the point $(23, -0.9)$. Which of the following can be concluded from this?

   A) A country with 23 adversaries cannot sell the export to other nations.
   B) A country with 23 adversaries cannot decrease its price any further.
   C) A country cannot have more than 22 adversaries.
   D) The line of best fit will not model the price of the export well for a country with many adversaries.

149. A country not shown in the scatterplot sells the export for $1525. If the country's price is more than that predicted by the line of best fit, what is the least number of adversaries the country can have?

   A) 1
   B) 2
   C) 3
   D) 4

150. Which of the following describes an exponential relationship between the pair of variables listed?

   A) Each second s, an airplane's speed r increases at a constant rate of 15 feet per second.
   B) For every 2-centimeter increase in the distance d from the insulated end of a metal rod, the temperature, T, of an object decreases by 3%.
   C) Each day d after a blizzard, the amount of snow on the ground, S, decreases by 2 pounds per cubic foot.
   D) For each increase x by 1 square foot, the price of a New York City apartment increases by $1200.

151.* John, a United States resident, is on vacation in Spain and is trying to decide if he should use his own credit card from the U.S., or to purchase a prepaid credit card for 500 euros in Spain.

The bank that issues John's U.S. credit card converts all purchase prices at the foreign exchange rate for that day, and an additional fee of 6% of the converted cost is applied before the bank posts the charge.

If John decides to purchase the prepaid card, he can use this card spending dollars at the exchange rate for that day with no fee, but he loses any money left unspent on the card.

Suppose that John does decide to buy the prepaid card. What is the least number of the 500 euros John must spend for the prepaid card to have been the cheaper option? Round your answer to the nearest whole number of euros.

152. For 5 numbers in a list of increasing numbers, the average (arithmetic mean), median, and mode are all equal to 11. The range of the list is 7. The second number in the list is less than 11 and 2 more than the least number in the list. What is the greatest number in the list?

5 6 7 8 9

LEVEL 5: GEOMETRY AND COMPLEX NUMBERS

153. A square is inscribed in a circle of diameter d. What is the perpendicular distance from the center of the circle to a side of the square, in terms of d ?

A) $\frac{d}{2}$

B) $\frac{d\sqrt{2}}{4}$

C) $\frac{d\sqrt{2}}{2}$

D) d

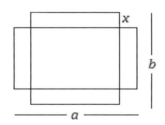

154. A square with sides of length x centimeters has been removed from each corner of a rectangular sheet of metal with length a and width b. The metal is then folded upward to form an open box. Which of the following quantities is equal to $2x(a + b - 4x)$?

A) The volume of the interior of the closed box
B) The surface area of the closed box
C) The area of the five faces of the box
D) The area of the four lateral faces of the box

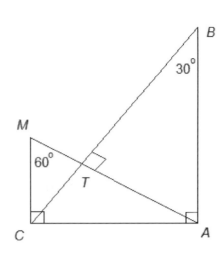

155. For the triangles in the figure above, which of the following ratios of side lengths is equivalent to the ratio of the perimeter of ΔCBA to the perimeter of ΔMAC ?

A) $AB:CA$
B) $AB:AM$
C) $AB:BC$
D) $AB:CM$

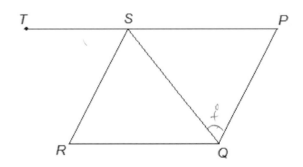

156. In the figure above, $\overline{QS}$ is the shorter diagonal of rhombus $PQRS$ and T is on $\overrightarrow{PS}$. The measure of angle PQS is $x°$. What is the measure of RST, in terms of x ?

A) $x°$
B) $2x°$
C) $(90 - x)°$
D) $(180 - 2x)°$

157. The circumference of the base of a right circular cone is 10π and the circumference of a parallel cross section is 8π. If the distance between the base and the cross section is 6, what is the height of the cone?

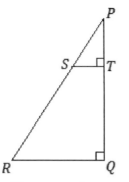

Note: Figure not drawn to scale.

158. In the figure above, $\cos P = \frac{12}{13}$. If $RQ = 10$ and $TQ = 3$, what is the length of $\overline{RS}$?

$$x^2 + y^2 - 3x + 5y - \frac{1}{2} = 0$$

159. The equation above defines a circle in the xy-plane. What is the <u>diameter</u> of the circle?

160. Let $x = 1 + i$, $y = 1 - i$, $z = 2 + 3i$, $w = \frac{x}{y}$, and $u = \frac{w}{z}$. When u is written in the form $a + bi$, what is the value of $13(a + b)$? (Note that $i = \sqrt{-1}$)

PROBLEMS BY LEVEL AND TOPIC
PROBLEM SET C

Full solutions to these problems are available for free download here:
www.SATPrepGet800.com/500SATx2

LEVEL 1: HEART OF ALGEBRA

1. If $\frac{10}{9}k = \frac{3}{5}$, what is the value of k ?

    A) $\frac{2}{3}$

    B) $\frac{27}{50}$

    C) $\frac{9}{25}$

    D) $\frac{1}{5}$

    [handwritten: $27 = 50k$]

    [handwritten: $\frac{27}{50} = k$]

2. A veterinarian charges a pet owner \$150 for an office visit, as well as \$50 for each test that needs to be run and \$30 for each medication that needs to be prescribed. Which of the following expressions best models the total cost, in dollars, to bring in a pet that requires t tests and m medications?

    A) $(50 + 30)(t + m)$
    B) $(50 + 30)(t + m) - 150$
    C) $(50 + 150)t + 30m$
    D) $150 + 50t + 30m$

3. Which of the following statements is true regarding the line with equation $y = -5$?

    A) The line is vertical.
    B) The line is horizontal.
    C) The line has a positive slope.
    D) The line has a negative slope.

$$20t + 5c = 240$$

4. Daniel is playing poker with some friends. The equation above can be used to model the number of chips, c, that Daniel still has in his possession t hours after he begins playing. What does it mean that $t = 0$, $c = 48$ is a solution to this equation?

    A) Daniel is losing 48 chips per hour.
    B) It would take 48 hours for Daniel to have 240 chips.
    C) Daniel can play for 48 hours before losing all his chips.
    D) Daniel begins playing with 48 chips.

$$F = \frac{9}{5}C + 32$$

5. The formula above shows how a temperature C, measured in degrees Celsius, relates to a temperature F, measured in degrees Fahrenheit. What is C in terms of F ?

   A) $C = \frac{5}{9}F + 32$

   B) $C = \frac{5}{9}F - 32$

   C) $C = \frac{5}{9}(F - 32)$

   D) $C = \frac{9}{5}F + 32$

$$x = 3 - y$$
$$5y = 15$$

6. Which of the following ordered pairs (x, y) satisfies the system of equations above?

   A) $(6, 3)$
   B) $(1, 2)$
   C) $(3, 0)$
   D) $(0, 3)$

7. If $3\left(\frac{x-4}{7}\right) = d$ and $d = 15$, what is the value of x ? 39

8. The function W defined by $W(a) = 1.9a + 2.3$ models the weight of a kitten, in ounces, that is a weeks old for $0 \leq a \leq 6$. According to this model, what is the weight, in ounces, of a kitten that is 3 weeks old? 8

LEVEL 1: PASSPORT TO ADVANCED MATH

9. If $f(x) = 2 - 5(x^2 + 1)$, which of the following is equivalent to $f(x)$?

   A) $3 - 5x^2$
   B) $-3 - 5x^2$
   C) $7 - 5x^2$
   D) $1 - 5x^2$

10. Which of the following graphs could not be the graph of a function?

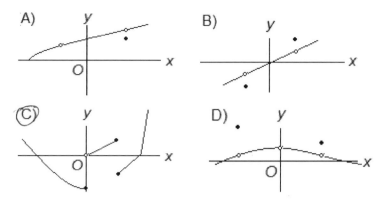

A)

B)

Ⓒ

D)

11. For which nonnegative value of k is the expression $\frac{1}{4-k^2}$ undefined?

A) 0
B) $\sqrt{2}$
Ⓒ 2
D) 4

$$y = 2x^2$$
$$x = 2y$$

12. Which value is a y-coordinate of a solution to the system of equations above?

A) 1
B) $\frac{1}{2}$
C) $\frac{1}{4}$
Ⓓ $\frac{1}{8}$

13. If $3a(2b + 5c) = jab + kac$, where $a, b, c, j,$ and k are constants, what is the value of jk ?

90

14. If $3^{x+1} = 27$, what is the value of x ? 2

15. If $x^2 = 3yz$, what is the value of $\frac{x^2}{yz}$? 3

16. If $c > 0$, for what value of c will $\frac{c^2+13}{7} = 11$? 8

LEVEL 1: PROBLEM SOLVING

17. The ratio of 29 to 5 is equal to the ratio of 203 to what number?

    A) $\frac{1}{35}$

    B) $\frac{5}{7}$

    C) $\frac{7}{5}$

    D) 35

18. A store owner buys and sells watches, always keeping track of how many watches he has available for sale in his store. This data is shown on the graph below.

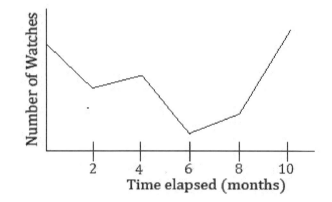

When did the store owner have the least number of watches?

    A) After 2 months
    B) After 4 months
    C) After 6 months
    D) After 8 months

Questions 19 - 22 refer to the following information.

Ten 25-year-old men were asked how many hours per week they exercise and their resting heart rate was taken in beats per minute (BPM). The results are shown as points in the scatterplot below, and the line of best fit is drawn.

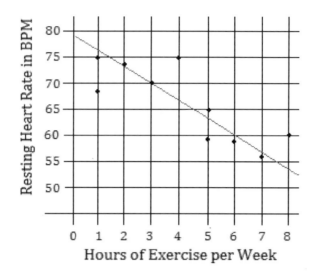

19. How many of the men have a resting heart rate that differs by more than 5 BPM from the resting heart rate predicted by the line of best fit?

    A) None
    B) Two
    C) Three
    D) Four

20. Based on the line of best fit, what is the predicted resting heart rate for someone that exercises three and a half hours per week?

    A) 66 BPM
    B) 68 BPM
    C) 70 BPM
    D) 72 BPM

21. What is the resting heart rate, in BPM, of the man represented by the data point that is farthest from the line of best fit?

    A) 60
    B) 66
    C) 68
    D) 75

22. Which of the following is the best interpretation of the slope of the line of best fit in the context of this problem?

   A) The predicted number of hours that a person must exercise to maintain a resting heart rate of 50 BPM
   B) The predicted resting heart rate of a person that does not exercise
   C) The predicted decrease in resting heart rate, in BPM, for each one hour increase in weekly exercise
   D) The predicted increase in the number of hours of exercise needed to increase the resting heart rate by one BPM

23. The mass of an object is equal to the product of the volume of the object and the density of the object. What is the density of an object, in kilograms per cubic meter, of an object with a mass of 40 kilograms and a volume of 10 cubic meters?

24. Dan, Craig, Phil, and John own a total of 37 paintings. If Dan owns 10 of them, what is the average (arithmetic mean) number of paintings owned by John, Craig, and Phil?

LEVEL 1: GEOMETRY AND COMPLEX NUMBERS

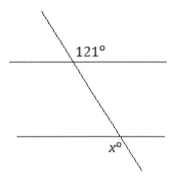

25. The figure above shows two parallel lines cut by a transversal. What is the value of x ?

   A) 31
   B) 59
   C) 121
   D) 239

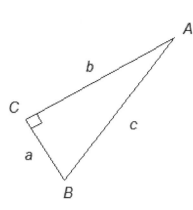

26. The dimensions of the right triangle above are given in meters. What is $\cos A$?

    A) $\dfrac{b}{a}$
    B) $\dfrac{b}{c}$
    C) $\dfrac{a}{b}$
    D) $\dfrac{c}{b}$

27. For $i = \sqrt{-1}$, which of the following is equivalent to $i + 2i^2$?

    A) $2 + i$
    B) $2 - i$
    C) $-2 + i$
    D) $-2 - i$

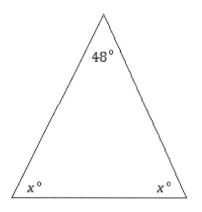

28. In the triangle above, what is the value of x ?

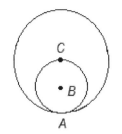

29. In the figure above, A, B, and C lie on the same line. B is the center of the smaller circle, and C is the center of the larger circle. If the radius of the smaller circle is 3, what is the diameter of the larger circle?

30. A pyramid has a rectangular base. The length of the base is 3 feet and the width of the base is 5 feet. If the height of the pyramid is 10 feet, what is the volume of the pyramid, in cubic feet?

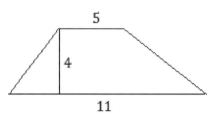

31. What is the area of the trapezoid shown above?

32. For $i = \sqrt{-1}$, when we add the complex numbers $5i$, $6 + i$, and $2 - 2i$, we get the complex number $a + bi$. What is the value of b ?

LEVEL 2: HEART OF ALGEBRA

33. Gina subscribes to a cell phone service that charges a monthly fee of \$60.00. The first 500 megabytes of data are free, and the cost is \$0.15 for each additional megabyte of data used that month. Which of the following functions gives the cost, in dollars, for a month in which Gina uses x megabytes of data, where $x > 500$?

    A) $60 + 15x$
    B) $0.15x - 15$
    C) $0.15x - 440$
    D) $60 + 0.15x$

34. The line $y = mx + b$, where m and b are constants, is graphed in the xy-plane. If the line contains the point (c, d) where c and d are nonzero, what is b in terms of c and d ?

    A) $d - mc$
    B) $d + mc$
    C) $\frac{d-m}{c}$
    D) $\frac{d-c}{m}$

35. Which of the following is the graph of the equation $y = -\frac{1}{2}x + 3$ in the xy-plane?

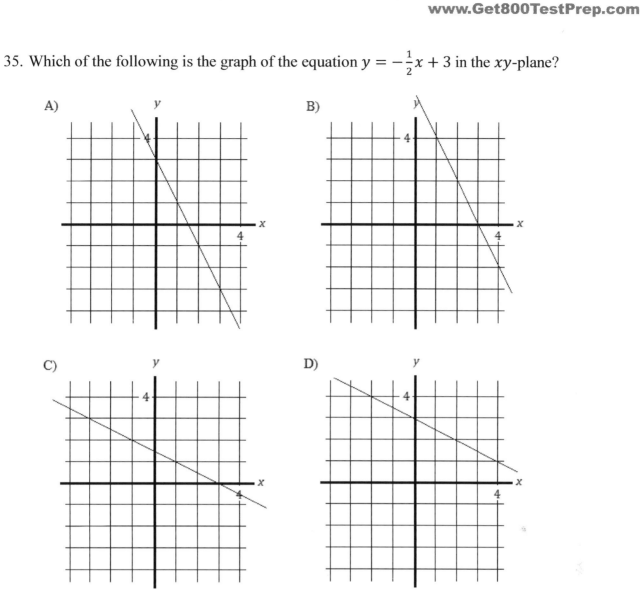

36. The graph of which of the following equations in the xy-plane is a line with slope -5 ?

    A) $y = -5x$

    B) $y = -\frac{1}{5}x$

    C) $y = \frac{1}{5}x$

    D) $y = 5x$

37. If $3x = 9y$, what is the value of $\frac{6y}{x}$?

38. A line is shown in the xy-plane above. A second line (not shown) is parallel to the line shown and passes through the points $(1, -5)$ and $(-7, k)$, where k is a constant. What is the value of k?

39. A florist is currently selling 12 different types of bouquets. The florist plans to introduce 3 new types of bouquets every year for the next 4 years. If an equation in the form $b = mt + k$ is used to represent the number of bouquets, b, that the florist will have available t years from now, what is the value of k?

$$52k + 34b = C$$

40. * The equation above gives the monthly cost C, in dollars, to take care of k kittens and b bunnies. John has 3 kittens and 5 bunnies, and Jenny has 2 kittens and 3 bunnies. How much greater, in dollars, is John's total cost than Jenny's total cost to take care of their respective pets? (Disregard the dollar sign when gridding your answer.)

LEVEL 2: PASSPORT TO ADVANCED MATH

$$7x^2 + 5x(3 - x) - 4(x - 2)$$

41. Which of the following polynomials is equivalent to the expression above?

A) $7x^2 - 10x - 8$
B) $7x^2 + 10x + 8$
C) $2x^2 + 11x + 8$
D) $2x^2 - 11x - 8$

42. Which of the following is equal to $b^{\frac{2}{3}}$ for all values of b ?

    A) $\sqrt[3]{b^2}$

    B) $\sqrt{b^3}$

    C) $\sqrt{b^{\frac{1}{3}}}$

    D) $\sqrt[3]{b^{\frac{1}{2}}}$

$$\sqrt{2b^2 + 21} - a = 0$$

43. If $a = 5$ in the equation above, which of the following is a possible value of b ?

    A) -2
    B) $-\sqrt{2}$
    C) 0
    D) 3

44. Suppose that $g(x) = 2x^2 - 5$, $g(k) = 45$, and $k > 0$. What is the value of k ?

45. The function f is defined by the equation $f(x) = 2^x - 3x + 1$. The point $(4, b)$ lies on the graph of f. What is the value of b?

46. If $\frac{5c}{d} = \frac{10}{3}$, what is the value of $\frac{d}{c}$?

47. The expression $(x^2 + 3) - (-2x^2 + x - 5)$ can be written in the form $ax^2 + bx + c$. What is the value of $a + b + c$?

48. What is the sum of the solutions to the equation $(x - 6)(x + 1.2) = 0$?

LEVEL 2: PROBLEM SOLVING

49. Each bundle of wires inside a large machine needs to be secured with 5 centimeters of electrical tape. What is the maximum number of these wire bundles that can be secured with 8 meters of electrical tape? (1 meter = 100 centimeters)

    A) 80
    B) 160
    C) 200
    D) 320

Questions 50 - 51 refer to the following information.

The table below shows the distribution of the five types of birds in an aviary.

Types of birds	Percent in aviary
Pelican	15%
Flamingo	8%
Water Thrush	25%
Stork	12%
Heron	40%

50. If a bird is selected at random from the aviary, what is the probability that the bird will NOT be a pelican?

   A) $\frac{3}{20}$

   B) $\frac{1}{4}$

   C) $\frac{2}{5}$

   D) $\frac{17}{20}$

51. If there are 60 more herons than pelicans in the aviary, what is the total number of birds in the aviary?

   A) 120
   B) 200
   C) 240
   D) 400

52. Which scatterplot shows a nonlinear positive association? (Note: A positive association between two variables is one in which higher values of one variable correspond to higher values of the other variable.)

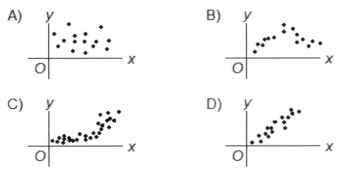

53. In 1980, an ounce of silver was worth $50. How heavy, in pounds, was $12,500 worth of silver in 1980? (16 ounces = 1 pound)

54. The weight of a liquid in a container is directly proportional to the volume of the liquid. Suppose that 4 gallons of a certain liquid weighs 5 pounds. What is the weight, in pounds, of 10 gallons of the same liquid?

55. * The *mina*, a Babylonian measure of weight, is approximately equal to 640 grams. It is also equivalent to 60 smaller Babylonian units called *talents*. Based on these relationships, 100 Babylonian talents is equivalent to how many <u>ounces,</u> to the nearest tenth? (28.35 grams = 1 ounce)

56. * What percent of 75 is 32 ? (Disregard the percent symbol when gridding in your answer.)

LEVEL 2: GEOMETRY AND COMPLEX NUMBERS

57. Violet is 5 feet tall and at a certain moment, the straight-line distance from the top of her head to the tip of her shadow is 13 feet. At this point in time, how long is violet's shadow?

    A) 8 feet.
    B) 9 feet
    C) 12 feet
    D) 14 feet

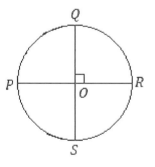

58. In the circle above with center O, $OR = 5$. What is the length of minor arc $\overset{\frown}{RS}$?

    A) $\frac{5\pi}{2}$
    B) $\frac{5\pi}{4}$
    C) $\frac{5\pi}{8}$
    D) $\frac{5\pi}{12}$

169

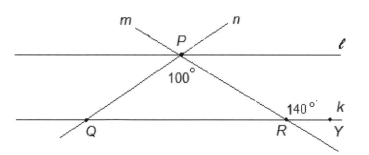

59. In the figure above, line ℓ is parallel to line k. Transversals m and n intersect at point P on ℓ and intersect k at points R and Q, respectively. Point Y is on k, the measure of $\angle PRY$ is 140°, and the measure of $\angle QPR$ is 100°. How many of the angles formed by rays ℓ, k, m, and n have measure 40° ?

    A) 4
    B) 6
    C) 8
    D) 10

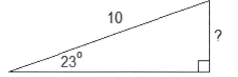

60. As shown above, a 10-foot ramp forms an angle of 23° with the ground, which is horizontal. Which of the following is an expression for the vertical rise, in feet, of the ramp?

    A) $10 \cos 23°$
    B) $10 \sin 23°$
    C) $10 \tan 23°$
    D) $10 \cot 23°$

61. If k is a positive integer, then i^{4k} must be equal to which of the following?

    A) 1
    B) −1
    C) i
    D) $-i$

62. The volume of a right circular cone is 72π cubic inches. If the height of the cone is equal to the base radius of the cone, what is the height of the cone, in inches?

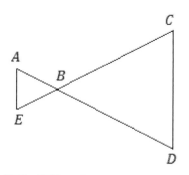

63. In the figure above, $\overline{AE} \parallel \overline{CD}$, $\overline{AB} \cong \overline{BE}$, and $m\angle ABE = 40°$. What is the measure, in degrees, of angle C ? (Disregard the degree sign when gridding in your answer.)

$$(x - 5)^2 + (y + 2)^2 = 9$$

64. The graph of the equation above in the xy-plane is a circle. What is the radius of the circle?

LEVEL 3: HEART OF ALGEBRA

65. During the second voyage of the HMS Beagle, Charles Darwin travelled from Plymouth Sound to Tenerife, stopping at Madeira along the way. The total distance he travelled during this part of his journey was 3275 miles, and the distance from Plymouth Sound to Madeira was 2657 miles more than the distance from Madeira to Tenerife. What was the distance from Madeira to Tenerif, in miles?

    A) 309
    B) 350
    C) 420
    D) 515

66. A line is graphed in the xy-plane. If the line has a negative slope and a positive y-intercept, which of the following points cannot lie on the line?

    A) $(-1, -1)$
    B) $(1, -1)$
    C) $(-1, 1)$
    D) $(1, 1)$

$$y = \frac{x}{2} - 5$$
$$x + \frac{y}{2} = \frac{5}{2}$$

67. Which of the following ordered pairs (x, y) satisfies the system of equations above?

    A) $(1, 3)$
    B) $(2, -4)$
    C) $(4, -3)$
    D) $(-3, 4)$

68. Last week, David slept 5 less hours than Gregory. If they slept a combined total of 99 hours, how many hours did Gregory sleep last week?

69. In 2012, Timothy had a collection consisting of 123 comic books. Starting in 2013, Timothy has been collecting 15 comic books per year. At this rate, in which year will Timothy first have had at least 141 comic books?

70. The line with the equation $\frac{2}{7}x + \frac{3}{5}y = 2$ is graphed in the xy-plane. What is the y-intercept of the line?

$$3x + y = 7$$
$$y = 2x - 1$$

71. In the solution (x, y) to the system of equations above, what is the value of y ?

72. The sum of two numbers is 50, and the difference when the smaller number is subtracted from the larger number is 10. What is the product of the two numbers?

LEVEL 3: PASSPORT TO ADVANCED MATH

$$f(x) = |2x - 3| - 1$$

73. For what positive value of x is $f(x)$ equal to 2 ?

    A) 0
    B) 2
    C) 3
    D) There is no such positive value of x.

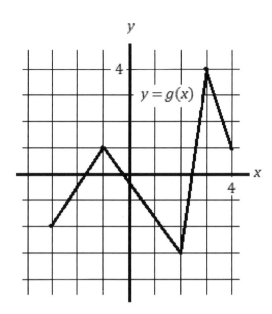

74. The entire graph of the function g is shown in the xy-plane above. Which of the following are equal to 7 ?

  I. $g(2) - g(3)$
 II. $g(3) - g(2)$
III. $g(2) + g(3)$

   A) I only
   B) II only
   C) III only
   D) II, and III only

75. In the xy-plane, the graph of function g has x-intercepts at -3, -1, and 3. Which of the following could define g ?

   A) $g(x) = (x - 3)^2(x - 1)^2$
   B) $g(x) = (x + 3)^2(x + 1)^2$
   C) $g(x) = (x - 3)^2(x + 1)(x + 3)$
   D) $g(x) = (x - 3)(x + 3)(x - 1)^2$

76. For a positive real number k, where $k^5 = 3$, what is the value of k^{10} ?

   A) 27
   B) 9
   C) 6
   D) $\sqrt{10}$

77. If $\frac{2d-3c}{3c} = \frac{2}{5}$, which of the following must also be true?

   A) $\frac{c}{d} = \frac{21}{10}$

   B) $\frac{c}{d} = \frac{10}{21}$

   C) $\frac{2d+3c}{3c} = \frac{21}{10}$

   D) $\frac{2d}{3c} = \frac{5}{7}$

78. Ohm's law states that the current I through a conductor between two points is found by dividing the voltage V across the two points by the resistance R of the conductor. Which of the following equations gives the voltage V in terms of I and R ?

   A) $V = I + R$

   B) $V = IR$

   C) $V = \frac{I}{R}$

   D) $V = \frac{R}{I}$

$$x^2 + 5 = \frac{5}{x^2 + 5}$$

79. In the equation above, which of the following is a possible value of $x^2 + 5$?

   A) 25

   B) 5

   C) $\sqrt{5}$

   D) $5 - \sqrt{5}$

$$x - 3 = \sqrt{3x - b}$$

80. If $b = 5$, what is the solution set of the equation above?

   A) $\{2\}$

   B) $\{7\}$

   C) $\{2,7\}$

   D) There are no solutions.

LEVEL 3: PROBLEM SOLVING

81. Laurie has three balls: a red ball, a blue ball, and a green ball. The weight of the red ball is approximately $\frac{11}{20}$ of the weight of the green ball, and the weight of the blue ball is approximately $\frac{27}{20}$ of the weight of the green ball. If the green ball weighs 30 pounds, approximately how many more pounds is the blue ball than the red ball?

    A) 16.5
    B) 24
    C) 31
    D) 40.4

x	1	2	3	4
y	$\frac{3}{2}$	$\frac{19}{6}$	$\frac{29}{6}$	$\frac{13}{2}$

82. Which of the following equations relates y to x for the values in the table above?

    A) $y = \frac{1}{6}x + \frac{4}{3}$
    B) $y = \frac{5}{3}x - \frac{1}{6}$
    C) $y = \frac{1}{3}\left(\frac{9}{2}\right)^x$
    D) $y = 3\left(\frac{1}{2}\right)^x$

Questions 83 - 86 refer to the following information.

Favorite Animals

	Dog	Cat	Elephant	Monkey	Lion	Total
Fresh	82	17	20	36	18	173
Soph	51	46	5	50	6	158
Jun	24	30	63	22	30	169
Total	157	93	88	108	54	500

The table above lists the results of a survey of a random sample of 500 high school freshman, sophomores, and juniors. Each student selected exactly one animal that was his or her favorite.

83. * If one of the freshman from the sample is selected at random, which of the following is closest to the percentage of students who selected the monkey as his or her favorite animal?

    A) 7%
    B) 21%
    C) 33%
    D) 50%

84. If one of the 500 students is selected at random, what is the probability that the student's favorite animal is an elephant or lion?

   A) $\frac{11}{500}$

   B) $\frac{27}{500}$

   C) $\frac{93}{500}$

   D) $\frac{71}{250}$

85. * If the sample is representative of a high school with 2,500 freshmen, sophomores and juniors, then based on the table, what is the predicted number of juniors at the high school who would select the elephant as their favorite animal?

   A) 63
   B) 88
   C) 315
   D) 845

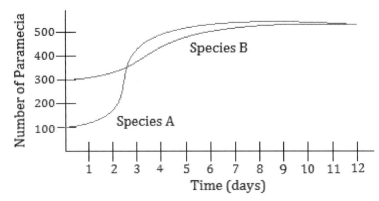

Paramecia present (in thousands) over twelve days

86. A small puddle is monitored by scientists for the number of *paramecia* present. The scientists are interested in two distinct species, let's call them "species *A*" and "species *B*." At time $t = 0$, the scientists measure and estimate the amount of species *A* and species *B* present in the puddle. They then proceed to measure and record the number of each species of *paramecium* present every hour for 12 days. The data for each species were then fit by a smooth curve, as shown in the graph above. Which of the following is a correct statement about the data above?

   A) At time $t = 0$, the number of species *B* present is 150% greater than the number of species *A* present.

   B) At time $t = 0$, the number of species *A* present is 75% less than the number of species *B* present.

   C) For the first 3 days, the average growth rate of species *B* is higher than the average growth rate of species *A*.

   D) The growth rate of both species *A* and species *B* decreases for the last 8 days.

87. The prom committee at a high school surveyed a random sample of 120 high school seniors to determine whether they should have an 80's or 90's themed prom. Of the students surveyed, 35% preferred to have a 90's themed prom. Based on this information, about how many students in the entire 300-person senior class would be expected to prefer having the prom with a 90's theme?

   A) 95
   B) 100
   C) 105
   D) 110

88. A group of colleagues plan to divide the $2400 cost of a business conference equally amongst themselves. When six of the colleagues decided not to attend the conference, those remaining still divided the $2400 cost equally, but each colleague's share of the cost increased by $90. How many colleagues were in the original group?

LEVEL 3: GEOMETRY AND COMPLEX NUMBERS

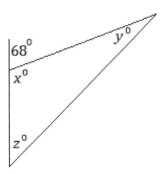

89. In the figure above, one side of a triangle is extended. Which of the following is true?

   A) $y = 68$
   B) $z = 68$
   C) $y + z = 68$
   D) $z - y = 68$

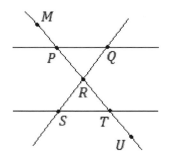

Note: Figure not drawn to scale.

90. In the figure above, $\angle MPQ \cong \angle STU$. Each of the following statements must be true EXCEPT

    A) $\overline{PQ} \parallel \overline{ST}$
    B) $m\angle MPQ + m\angle RTS = 180°$
    C) $\triangle PQR \sim \triangle TSR$
    D) $\triangle PQR \cong \triangle TSR$

91. If each side length of a rectangle is doubled, how would the area of the rectangle change?

    A) The area would be multiplied by 4.
    B) The area would be multiplied by 2.
    C) The area would not change.
    D) The area would be cut in half.

92. If $i = \sqrt{-1}$, which of the following complex numbers is equivalent to $(-7 - 3i)(5 - i)$?

    A) $-35 + 3i$
    B) $-35 - 3i$
    C) $-32 - 8i$
    D) $-38 - 8i$

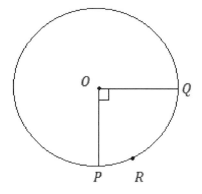

93. In the circle above with center O, $\angle POQ$ is a right angle. If the length of arc $\overset{\frown}{PRQ}$ is 10π, what is the length of a <u>diameter</u> of the circle?

94. * A heptagon is a polygon with 7 sides and 7 angles. What is the degree measure of an interior angle of a regular heptagon, to the nearest degree? (Disregard the degree symbol when gridding your answer.)

95. * A crystal shaped like a pyramid has a rectangular base such that the length of the base is $\frac{1}{3}$ the width of the base and the height is twice the length of the base. If the volume of the pyramid is 250 cubic inches, what is the height of the pyramid, in inches?

96. A circle with center $(1, 4)$ lies in the xy-plane. The circle has x-intercepts $(4, 0)$ and $(-2, 0)$. What is the radius of the circle?

LEVEL 4: HEART OF ALGEBRA

97. Joseph joins a gym that charges $79.99 per month plus tax for a premium membership. A tax of 6% is applied to the monthly fee. Joseph is also charged a one-time initiation fee of $95 as soon as he joins. There is no contract so that Joseph can cancel at any time without having to pay a penalty. Which of the following represents Joseph's total charge, in dollars, if he keeps his membership for t months?

   A) $1.06(79.99 + 95)t$
   B) $1.06(79.99t + 95)$
   C) $1.06(79.99t) + 95$
   D) $(79.99 + 0.06t) + 95$

98. The graph of $y = g(x)$ is a line in the xy-plane with slope 7. Given that $g(-8) = 11$, which of the following could be the definition of $g(x)$?

   A) $g(x) = 7x$
   B) $g(x) = 7x + 67$
   C) $g(x) = 7x - 67$
   D) $g(x) = 7x + 45$

$$2x + 5y = 3$$

99. The graph of the equation above is a line in the xy-plane. In which of the following equivalent forms of the equation does the y-intercept appear as a constant or coefficient?

   A) $5y = 3 - 2x$
   B) $x = \frac{3}{2} - \frac{5}{2}y$
   C) $y = \frac{3}{5} - \frac{2}{5}x$
   D) $2x - 5y - 3 = 0$

$$3x + y = 20$$
$$2x - 0.5y = 21.5$$

100. The solution to the system of equations above is (x, y). What is the value of y ?

    A) -7
    B) 5
    C) 9
    D) 63

101. A hospital manager will purchase first aid supplies and new machinery. The hospital has $75,000 left in its budget for the month. Each first aid kit costs the hospital $15 and each new piece of machinery costs the hospital $1200. Additionally, there is room for only 45 new pieces of machinery in the hospital. If k represents the number of first aid kits and m represents the number of pieces of machinery, which of the following systems of inequalities models this situation?

    A) $15k + 1200m \geq 75,000$
        $1 \leq k + m \leq 45$

    B) $15k + 1200m \geq 75,000$
        $1 \leq m \leq 45$
        $k \geq 1$

    C) $15k + 1200m \leq 75,000$
        $1 \leq k + m \leq 45$

    D) $15k + 1200m \leq 75,000$
        $1 \leq m \leq 45$
        $k \geq 1$

102. If $-\frac{27}{10} < 2 - 5x < -\frac{13}{5}$, then what is one possible value of $20x - 8$?

Cost of Coffee

Year	Price
1990	$0.15
1995	$0.28

103. The table above shows the price of coffee at a small coffee shop in Nebraska, for the years 1990 and 1995. If the relationship between coffee price and year is linear, which of the following functions C models the cost of coffee in dollars at this coffee shop t years after 1990 ?

    A) $C(t) = 0.15 + 0.026t$
    B) $C(t) = 0.15 + 0.26t$
    C) $C(t) = 0.15 + 0.026(t - 1990)$
    D) $C(t) = 0.15 + 0.26(t - 1990)$

104. A group of 51 people went on a canoeing excursion. A total of 23 canoes were used. Some of the canoes held 3 people, and the rest of the canoes held 2 people. Assuming all 23 of the canoes were filled to capacity and every person in the group participated in the excursion, exactly how many 3-person canoes were there?

LEVEL 4: PASSPORT TO ADVANCED MATH

8/15/19

105. Which of the following expressions is equivalent to $(9x^7y^5)^{\frac{1}{2}}$, for x and y nonnegative?

A) $3x^{\frac{7}{2}}y^{\frac{5}{2}}$

B) $3x^{\sqrt{7}}y^5$

C) $\frac{9}{2}x^{\frac{7}{2}}y^5$

D) $\frac{9}{2}x^{\sqrt{7}}y^{\frac{5}{2}}$

$3x^3\sqrt{x}\ y^2\sqrt{y}$

$$\frac{7}{x+3} + \frac{6}{3(x+3)}$$

106. Which of the following expressions is equivalent to the one above, where $x \neq -3$?

A) $\frac{27}{3x+9}$

B) $\frac{16}{3x+9}$

C) $\frac{13}{x+3}$

D) $\frac{9}{x+3}$

107. Which of the following is the set of x-values that are solutions to the quadratic equation $5x^2 + 15x - 50 = 0$?

A) $\{-2, -5\}$
B) $\{-2, 5\}$
C) $\{2, -5\}$
D) $\{2, 5\}$

108. What are the solutions to $x^2 - 5 = x$?

A) $x = \frac{-1\pm\sqrt{29}}{2}$

B) $x = \frac{-1\pm\sqrt{21}}{2}$

C) $x = \frac{1\pm\sqrt{29}}{2}$

D) $x = \frac{1\pm\sqrt{21}}{2}$

$$h(t) = -16t^2 + bt + c$$

109. In the function above, b and c are positive constants. The function models the height h, in feet, of an object above ground level t seconds after being thrown straight up in the air. What does the constant c represent in the function?

    A) The initial speed, in feet per second, of the object
    B) The maximum speed, in feet per second, of the object
    C) The initial height, in feet, of the object
    D) The maximum height, in feet, of the object

110. If $\frac{2k+3}{3k-1} = 2$, what is the value of k ?

111. If $5 + 4x^2 = 5x^2 - 9x + 25$, what is one possible value of x ?

112. If $(x + 3)^2 - 10(x + 3) + 25 = 0$, what is the value of x ?

LEVEL 4: PROBLEM SOLVING

113. 100 residents from a particular city were chosen at random and asked if they had pets. 45 of them reported that they did have pets. If the reported percentage is used as an estimate for the proportion of all residents in the town who have pets, the margin of error is 11%. Which of the following is the most appropriate conclusion based on the data provided?

    A) Between 0% and 34% of all the residents in the city have pets.
    B) Between 34% and 56% of all the residents of the city have pets.
    C) Approximately 33% of all the residents in the city have pets.
    D) 45% of all the residents in the city have pets.

Questions 114 - 117 refer to the following information.

The scatterplot below shows the number of people diagnosed with melanoma, in ten-thousands, from 1940 to 1970.

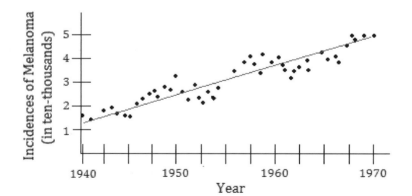

114. Based on the data shown in the figure, in 1969, approximately how many incidences of melanoma were there?

    A) 5
    B) 5000
    C) 40,000
    D) 50,000

115. According to the line of best fit, which of the following best approximates the year in which the number of incidences of melanoma was estimated to be 20,000 ?

    A) 1942
    B) 1946
    C) 1950
    D) 1954

116. Based on the line of best fit to the data, as shown in the figure, which of the following values is closest to the average yearly increase in the number of incidences of melanoma?

    A) 1,300
    B) 330
    C) 0.33
    D) 0.13

117. Based on the data shown in the figure, which of the following values is closest to the range of the number of incidences of melanoma between 1945 and 1950 ?

    A) 5,000
    B) 10,000
    C) 17,000
    D) 36,000

118. On January 1, 2015, a family living on an island releases their two pet rabbits into the wild. Due to the short gestation period of rabbits, and the fact that the rabbits have no natural predators on this island, the rabbit population doubles each month. If P represents the rabbit population t years after January 1, 2015, then which of the following equations best models the rabbit population on this island over time?

    A) $P = 2^{\frac{t+12}{12}}$
    B) $P = 2^{t+1}$
    C) $P = 2^{12t}$
    D) $P = 2^{12t+1}$

Questions 119 – 120 refer to the following information.

Fabric	Cost per square foot in US dollars	Cost per square foot in British pounds
Cotton	0.41	0.31
Wool	0.66	0.50
Silk	1.17	0.89

The table above gives the typical cost per square foot of several fabrics in both US dollars and British pounds on November 1, 2017.

119.* The ratio of the cost of cotton per square foot in British pounds to the cost of cotton per square foot in US dollars is $b : 1$, where b is a constant. What is the value of b, rounded to the nearest hundredth?

120.* What percent of the cost of silk in US dollars is the cost of wool in US dollars? (Disregard the percent symbol when gridding your answer.)

LEVEL 4: GEOMETRY AND COMPLEX NUMBERS

121. In $\triangle DOG$, the measure of $\angle D$ is 60° and the measure of $\angle O$ is 30°. If $\overline{DO}$ is 8 units long, what is the area, in square units, of $\triangle DOG$?

A) 4
B) 8
C) $8\sqrt{2}$
D) $8\sqrt{3}$

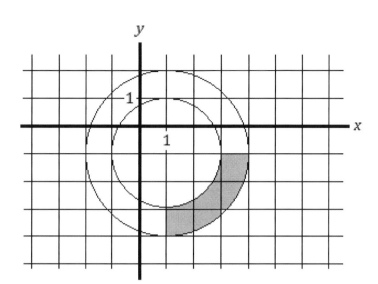

122. Two circles are drawn in the xy-plane above. Both circles have center $(1, -1)$ and their diameters are 4 and 6, respectively. What is the area of the shaded region?

A) $\frac{5\pi}{4}$

B) $\frac{5\pi}{2}$

C) $\frac{25\pi}{8}$

D) 5π

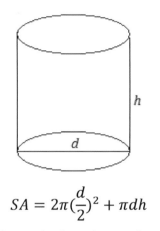

$$SA = 2\pi\left(\frac{d}{2}\right)^2 + \pi dh$$

123. The formula above can be used to calculate the total surface area of the right circular cylinder shown, where h is the height of the cylinder, and d is the diameter of each circular base. What must the expression πdh represent?

A) The area of a circular base
B) The sum of the areas of the two circular bases
C) The lateral surface area
D) The sum of the area of one circular base and the lateral surface area

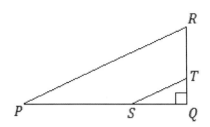

124. In the figure above, $\overline{ST} \parallel \overline{PR}$, $PS = 5$ and $SQ = 2$. What is the ratio of the length of segment $\overline{ST}$ to the length of segment $\overline{PR}$?

    A) $2:5$
    B) $2:6$
    C) $2:7$
    D) $3:7$

125. If the side length of a rhombus is doubled, how would the area of the rhombus change?

    A) The area would be multiplied by 4.
    B) The area would be multiplied by 2.
    C) The area would not change.
    D) The area would be cut in half.

126. Acute angles A and B satisfy $\sin A = \cos B$. If $m\angle A = (3d - 5)°$ and $m\angle B = (2d - 7)°$, what is the value of d ?

127. A line segment is drawn from the center of a 15-sided regular polygon to each vertex of the polygon forming 15 isosceles triangles. What is the measure of a base angle of one of these triangles? (Disregard the degree symbol when gridding your answer.)

128. * If $i = \sqrt{-1}$, and $\frac{(2-3i)}{(i-7)} = a + bi$, where a and b are real numbers, then what is the value of $|a|$ to the nearest tenth?

LEVEL 5: HEART OF ALGEBRA

129. A paleontologist estimates the weight of a new dinosaur species to be w tons, where $w > 20$. For an experiment to be successful, the paleontologist needs his estimate to be within 2 tons of the actual weight of the dinosaur. If the experiment is successful and the actual weight of the dinosaur is z tons, which of the following inequalities gives the relationship between the actual weight of the dinosaur and the paleontologist's estimate?

    A) $w > z + 2$
    B) $z > w + 2$
    C) $w - z < 2$
    D) $-2 < z - w < 2$

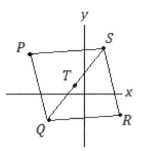

Note: Figure not drawn to scale.

130. In the xy-plane above, point T is the center of the square $PQRS$. The coordinates of points S and T are $(2, 5)$ and $(-1, 1)$, respectively. Which of the following is an equation of the line that passes through points P and R ?

A) $y = 1$

B) $y = -\dfrac{3}{4}x + 1$

C) $y = \dfrac{3}{4}x - \dfrac{1}{4}$

D) $y = -\dfrac{3}{4}x + \dfrac{1}{4}$

131. If $15 - 5x < -7$, which inequality represents the possible range of values of $6x - 18$?

A) $\dfrac{42}{5} < 6x - 18$

B) $\dfrac{42}{5} > 6x - 18$

C) $\dfrac{32}{5} < 6x - 18$

D) $\dfrac{32}{5} > 6x - 18$

132. An x% saline solution is a mixture of salt and water consisting of x% salt. Jessie wants to make a mixture of no more than 5 quarts from a 3% solution, a 7% solution, and a 12% solution to get a solution consisting of at least 10% salt. Let x be the number of quarts of the 3% solution, let y be the number of quarts of the 7% solution, and let z be the number of quarts of the 12% solution in the mixture. Which of the following systems represents all the constraints that x, y, and z must satisfy?

A) $\begin{cases} 0 < x < 5 \\ 0 < y < 5 \\ 0 < z < 5 \\ \frac{3x+7y+12z}{x+y+z} \geq 10 \end{cases}$

B) $\begin{cases} x > 0 \\ y > 0 \\ z > 0 \\ x + y + z \leq 5 \\ 3x + 7y + 12z \geq 10(x + y + z) \end{cases}$

C) $\begin{cases} x > 0 \\ y > 0 \\ z > 0 \\ x + y + z \leq 5 \\ 3x + 7y + 12z \geq 10 \end{cases}$

D) $\begin{cases} x > 0 \\ y > 0 \\ z > 0 \\ x + y + z = 5 \\ 3x + 7y + 12z \leq 10 \end{cases}$

$$x + 3y \geq -3$$
$$5x - 7y \leq 35$$

133. In the xy-plane, if a point with coordinates (a, b) lies in the solution set of the system of inequalities above, what is the maximum possible value of b?

A) $-\frac{25}{11}$

B) $\frac{25}{11}$

C) $\frac{42}{11}$

D) There is no maximum value for b.

x	$L(x)$
-3	8
1	16
5	24

134. Some values of the linear function L are shown in the table above. What is $L(-2)$?

$$4x = 3y - 1$$
$$7y = 5x + 3$$

135. (a, b) are the coordinates of the point of intersection of the two lines in the plane that are the graphs of the equations given above. What is the value of b ?

$$ax - 5y = c$$
$$3x + by = 7$$

136. In the system of equations above, a, b, and c are constants. If the two equations represent the same line, what is the value of ab^2c ?

LEVEL 5: PASSPORT TO ADVANCED MATH

137. For a polynomial $g(x)$, the value of $g(-3)$ is 2. Which of the following must be true about $g(x)$?

A) $x - 5$ is a factor of $g(x)$.
B) $x - 2$ is a factor of $g(x)$.
C) The remainder when $g(x)$ is divided by $x + 3$ is 2.
D) The remainder when $g(x)$ is divided by $x - 3$ is 2.

138. Which of the following is an equivalent form of $\sqrt[4]{x^{12m}y^3}$, where x and y are both positive?

A) $x^{3m}y^{\frac{3}{4}}$
B) $x^{4m}y^{-1}$
C) $x^{\frac{1}{2m}}y^{\frac{4}{3}}$
D) $x^{\frac{1}{3m}}y^{-1}$

$$h(x) = (x - 3)(x + 7)$$

139. Which of the following is an equivalent form of the function h above in which the minimum value of h appears as a coefficient or constant?

A) $h(x) = x^2 - 21$
B) $h(x) = x^2 + 4x - 21$
C) $h(x) = (x - 2)^2 - 21$
D) $h(x) = (x + 2)^2 - 25$

140. Let $f(x) = \frac{1}{3}(x-3)^2 + 2$ and $g(x) = 3x - 13$. What is one possible value of c such that $f(c) = g(c)$?

141. If the expression $\frac{x^3 - 5x^2 + 3x + 9}{x-1}$ is written in the equivalent form $ax^2 + bx + c + \frac{d}{x-1}$, what is the value of d ?

142. The expression $|3 - 8x| > 34$ is equivalent to $x < a$ or $x > b$. What is the value of $b - a$?

$$f(x) = 2x^2 - 18x + 12$$

143. Let a be the product of the roots of the function f shown above, and let b be the sum of the roots of f. What is the value of $\frac{a}{b}$?

$$2x^2 - y^2 = 16$$
$$2x - y = 4$$

144. If (x, y) is a solution to the system of equations above, what is the value of x ?

LEVEL 5: PROBLEM SOLVING

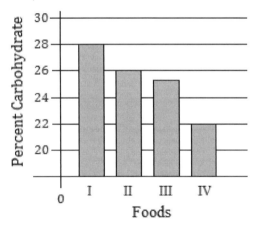

Percent Carbohydrate in Four Foods

145. * The graph above shows the amount of carbohydrate supplied by four different foods, I, II, III, and IV, as a percentage of their total weights. The cost of 20 ounces of foods I, II, III, and IV, are \$4.00, \$3.50, \$3.00, and \$2.75, respectively. Which of the four foods supplies the most carbohydrate per dollar?

A) I
B) II
C) III
D) IV

190

146. Suppose that the average (arithmetic mean) of a, b, and c is h, the average of b, c, and d is j, and the average of d and e is k. What is the average of a and e ?

    A) $h - j + k$

    B) $\frac{3h+3j-2k}{2}$

    C) $\frac{3h-3j+2k}{2}$

    D) $\frac{3h-3j+2k}{5}$

147. To determine if exercising regularly reduces the risk of diabetes in women, scientists interviewed a random sample of 8,000 women who had no family history of diabetes. Participants in the study were identified as occasional or regular exercisers. Ten years later, the scientists found that the proportion of women with diabetes was significantly lower for the women identified as regular exercisers. Which of the following is the most reasonable conclusion?

    A) Exercising regularly reduces the risk of diabetes in women, but not necessarily in men.
    B) Exercising regularly reduces the risk of diabetes in both women and men.
    C) There is an association between exercising regularly and the risk of diabetes for women, but it is not necessarily a cause-and-effect relationship, and the association may not exist for men.
    D) There is an association between exercising regularly and the risk of diabetes for women and men, but it is not necessarily a cause-and-effect relationship.

148. A rectangle was changed by increasing its length by r percent and decreasing its width by 20%. If these changes increased the area of the rectangle by 4%, what is the value of r ?

    A) 10
    B) 20
    C) 30
    D) 40

149.* A survey was conducted among a randomly chosen sample of 250 single men and 250 single women about whether they owned any dogs or cats. The table below displays a summary of the survey results.

	Dogs Only	Cats Only	Both	Neither	Total
Men	92	27	5	126	250
Women	75	43	34	98	250
Total	167	70	39	224	500

According to the table, which of the following statements is most likely to be false?

A) The probability that a woman is a cat owner is greater than the probability that a cat owner is a woman

B) The probability that a dog owner is male is greater than the probability that a randomly chosen person is a cat owner.

C) The probability that a woman does not own a dog or cat is greater than the probability that a man owns at least one dog and one cat.

D) The probability that a cat owner is a woman is greater than the probability that a man owns a dog.

$$S = 161{,}400 \left(1 + \frac{16.9}{100}\right)^t$$

150. The mean annual salary of an NBA player, S, can be estimated using the equation above, where S is measured in thousands of dollars, and t represents the number of years since 1980 for $0 \leq t \leq 20$. Which of the following statements is the best interpretation of 16.9 in the context of this problem?

A) The estimated mean annual salary, in dollars, of an NBA player in 1980.
B) The estimated mean annual salary, in dollars, of an NBA player in 2000.
C) The estimated yearly increase in the mean annual salary of an NBA player.
D) The estimated yearly percent increase in the mean annual salary of an NBA player.

Questions 151 - 152 refer to the following information.

A biologist places a colony consisting of 5000 bacteria into a petri dish. After the initial placement of the bacteria at time $t = 0$, the biologist measures and estimates the number of bacteria present every half hour. This data was then fitted by an exponential curve of the form $y = c \cdot 2^{kt}$ where c and k are constants, t is measured in hours, and y is measured in thousands of bacteria. The scatterplot together with the exponential curve are shown below.

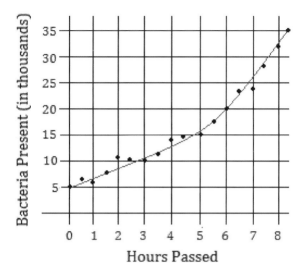

151. According to the scatterplot, the biologist's measurements indicate that the number of bacteria present quadrupled in 6 hours, and the exponential curve passes through the corresponding data point at time $t = 6$. The exponential function also agrees with the initial number of bacteria. What is the value of ck ?

152. Suppose that the data was fitted with a quadratic function of the form $t^2 + bt + c$ instead of an exponential function. Assume that the quadratic function agrees with the scatterplot at times $t = 0$ and $t = 6$. What is the t-coordinate of the vertex of the graph of the quadratic function?

193

LEVEL 5: GEOMETRY AND COMPLEX NUMBERS

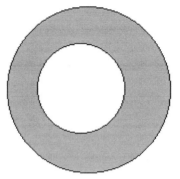

153. A circular disk is cut out of a larger circular disk, as shown in the figure above, so that the area of the piece that remains is the same as the area of the cutout. If the radius of the larger circle is R, what is the circumference of the cutout, in terms of R ?

    A) $R\pi$
    B) $R\sqrt{2}$
    C) $R\pi\sqrt{2}$
    D) $2R\pi\sqrt{2}$

154. A right circular cylinder has a base diameter of 4 and height 7. If point O is the center of the top of the cylinder and B lies on the circumference of the bottom of the cylinder, what is the straight-line distance between O and B ?

    A) 3
    B) 7
    C) 11
    D) $\sqrt{53}$

155. * Jonathon wants to place a rectangular fence around the border to his backyard. The width of the fence will be 350 inches more than 5 times the length of the fence. What will be the perimeter of Jonathon's fence if the area of the fence is 64,680 square inches?

    A) 854 inches
    B) 1274 inches
    C) 1708 inches
    D) 2548 inches

156. It is given that $\cos x = k$, where x is the radian measure of an angle and $\pi < x < \frac{3\pi}{2}$. If $\cos z = -k$, which of the following could <u>not</u> be the value of z ?

    A) $x - \pi$
    B) $\pi - x$
    C) $2\pi - x$
    D) $3\pi - x$

157. Let $i = \sqrt{-1}$, $z = a + bi$, and $\bar{z} = a - bi$. We define the absolute value of z to be $|z| = \sqrt{z\bar{z}}$. Which of the following is true?

    A) $|z|$ is always a nonnegative real number.
    B) $|z|$ is always a real number that can be positive, negative, or zero.
    C) $|z|$ is never a real number.
    D) $|z|$ can be real or complex.

158. A rectangular prism has a length that is 4 centimeters less than its height, and a width that is 4 centimeters more than its height. If the volume of the prism is 120 cubic centimeters, what is the surface area of the prism, in square centimeters?

$$\cos x = \sin(c - x)$$

159. In the equation above, $0 \le c < 2\pi$. If c and x are given in radians, what is one possible value of c, to the nearest tenth?

160. * The graph of $x^2 - 7x + y^2 - 13y - 14 = 0$ in the xy-plane is a circle. To the nearest tenth, what is the radius of the circle?

ANSWER KEY
PROBLEM SET A

1. A	33. C	65. B	97. C	129. A
2. D	34. C	66. C	98. D	130. D
3. C	35. B	67. D	99. C	131. C
4. D	36. A	68. D	100. D	132. B
5. C	37. C	69. 21	101. C	133. B
6. 1/2 , .5	38. D	70. 11/5, 2.2	102. 23	134. C
7. 6, 7, 8, 9	39. 1/2, .5	71. 3/5, .6	103. 32	135. 20/3, 6.66,
8. 35	40. 1	72. 2/3 , .666,	104. 15	6.67
9. C	41. C	.667	105. C	136. 1.36
10. D	42. 2	73. A	106. B	137. B
11. C	43. B	74. C	107. C	138. A
12. D	44. C	75. A	108. D	139. D
13. D	45. C	76. A	109. D	140. B
14. 13	46. 7	77. C	110. 1	141. A
15. 1	47. 2/3, .666,	78. B	111. 4/3 , 1.33	142. 24, 32, 48,
16. 0	.667	79. C	112. 5/3, 1.66,	128, 4096
17. D	48. 5	80. 5/3, 1.66,	1.67	143. 30
18. B	49. B	1.67	113. A	144. 36
19. C	50. A	81. C	114. B	145. C
20. C	51. B	82. B	115. C	146. D
21. B	52. 21	83. C	116. A	147. A
22. 45	53. 72	84. B	117. D	148. C
23. 4000	54. .358, .359	85. D	118. C	149. A
24. 8	55. 30	86. B	119. D	150. B
25. B	56. 150	87. .88	120. 6	151. B
26. C	57. B	88. 557	121. B	152. 2
27. D	58. D	89. B	122. A	153. D
28. D	59. B	90. D	123. C	154. B
29. C	60. B	91. D	124. 27.5, 55/2	155. C
30. 50	61. 125	92. 48	125. 140	156. B
31. 8	62. 10	93. 3	126. 3, 6, 9, 18	157. B
32. 81	63. 7/2, 3.5	94. 3/8, .375	127. 5/3, 1.66,	158. A
	64. 12/5, 2.4	95. 120	1.67	159. .493, .494
		96. 13	128. 1.31	160. 0

ANSWER KEY
PROBLEM SET B

1. D	33. C	65. D	97. B	129. B
2. C	34. B	66. B	98. C	130. C
3. A	35. C	67. D	99. C	131. C
4. C	36. A	68. B	100. C	132. 5/4, 1.25
5. B	37. D	69. C	101. 8	133. 84
6. 10	38. 553	70. B	102. 10	134. 71
7. 7	39. 1.06, 1.07	71. 1/2, .5	103. 3/2, 1.5	135. $0 < y < .04$
8. 4	40. 6	72. 10	104. 17	136. 2
9. A	41. A	73. C	105. D	137. D
10. B	42. A	74. D	106. A	138. B
11. A	43. C	75. B	107. D	139. C
12. A	44. B	76. B	108. A	140. C
13. 3	45. C	77. C	109. C	141. 5
14. 0	46. D	78. B	110. 1.7	142. 3/7, .428, .429
15. 4	47. 1, 1.41	79. 8	111. 12	143. 12
16. 42	48. 74	80. 2	112. 3/2, 1.5	144. 17
17. D	49. B	81. 3200	113. C	145. B
18. D	50. B	82. 1952	114. C	146. C
19. B	51. C	83. A	115. B	147. B
20. D	52. C	84. A	116. B	148. D
21. C	53. B	85. A	117. B	149. D
22. 1, 4, 7	54. 4.32	86. .7	118. 2/5, .4	150. B
23. 252	55. 2	87. 1878	119. 4.5	151. 472
24. 36	56. 89	88. 1760	120. 2/15, .133	152. 15
25. C	57. B	89. A	121. D	153. B
26. C	58. B	90. B	122. D	154. D
27. A	59. 10	91. B	123. D	155. A
28. 115	60. .2	92. C	124. D	156. D
29. 49.5, 99/2	61. 600	93. D	125. 120	157. 30
30. 3	62. 54	94. 101	126. 4	158. 13/4, 3.25
31. 144	63. .8, 4/5	95. 2.36	127. 5	159. 6
32. 7/25, .28	64. 1	96. 3	128. 1/2, .5	160. 5

ANSWER KEY
PROBLEM SET C

1. B	33. B	65. A	97. C	129. D
2. D	34. A	66. A	98. B	130. D
3. B	35. D	67. C	99. C	131. A
4. D	36. A	68. 52	100. A	132. B
5. C	37. 2	69. 2014	101. D	133. D
6. D	38. 3	70. 10/3, 3.33	102. 10.5, 10.6,	134. 10
7. 39	39. 12	71. 11/5, 2.2	10.7, 21/2,	135. 7/13, .538
8. 8	40. 120	72. 600	53/5	136. 525
9. B	41. C	73. C	103. A	137. C
10. C	42. A	74. B	104. 5	138. A
11. C	43. B	75. C	105. A	139. D
12. D	44. 5	76. B	106. A	140. 6, 9
13. 90	45. 5	77. B	107. C	141. 8
14. 2	46. 3/2, 1.5	78. B	108. D	142. 17/2 , 8.5
15. 3	47. 10	79. C	109. C	143. 2/3, .666,
16. 8	48. 28/5, 4.8	80. B	110. 5/4, 1.25	.667
17. D	49. B	81. B	111. 4, 5	144. 4
18. C	50. D	82. B	112. 2	145. C
19. C	51. C	83. B	113. B	146. C
20. B	52. C	84. D	114. D	147. A
21. C	53. 15.6	85. C	115. B	148. C
22. C	54. 25/2, 12.5	86. D	116. A	149. A
23. 4	55. 37.6	87. C	117. C	150. D
24. 9	56. 42.6, 42.7	88. 16	118. D	151. 5/3, 1.66
25. C	57. C	89. C	119. .76	1.67
26. B	58. A	90. D	120. 56.4	152. 7/4, 1.75
27. C	59. C	91. A	121. D	153. C
28. 66	60. B	92. D	122. A	154. D
29. 12	61. A	93. 40	123. C	155. C
30. 50	62. 6	94. 129	124. C	156. C
31. 32	63. 70	95. 10	125. A	157. A
32. 4	64. 3	96. 5	126. 20.4	158. 184
			127. 78	159. 1.6
			128. 3/10, .3	160. 8.3

ACTIONS TO COMPLETE AFTER YOU HAVE READ THIS BOOK

1. Take another practice SAT

You should see a substantial improvement in your score.

2. Continue to practice SAT math problems for 10 to 20 minutes each day

You may want to purchase *320 SAT Math Problems arranged by Topic and Difficulty Level* for additional practice problems.

3. 'Like' my Facebook page

This page is updated regularly with SAT prep advice, tips, tricks, strategies, and practice problems. Visit the following webpage and click the 'like' button.

www.facebook.com/SATPrepGet800

4. Review this book

If this book helped you, please post your positive feedback on the site you purchased it from; e.g. Amazon, Barnes and Noble, etc.

5. Claim your FREE bonuses

If you have not done so yet, visit the following webpage and enter your email address to receive solutions to all the supplemental problems in this book and other materials.

www.SATPrepGet800.com/500SATx2

About the Author

Dr. Steve Warner, a New York native, earned his Ph.D. at Rutgers University in Pure Mathematics in May 2001. While a graduate student, Dr. Warner won the TA Teaching Excellence Award.

After Rutgers, Dr. Warner joined the Penn State Mathematics Department as an Assistant Professor. In September 2002, Dr. Warner returned to New York to accept an Assistant Professor position at Hofstra University. By September 2007, Dr. Warner had received tenure and was promoted to Associate Professor. He has taught undergraduate and graduate courses in Precalculus, Calculus, Linear Algebra, Differential Equations, Mathematical Logic, Set Theory and Abstract Algebra.

Over that time, Dr. Warner participated in a five-year NSF grant, "The MSTP Project," to study and improve mathematics and science curriculum in poorly performing junior high schools. He also published several articles in scholarly journals, specifically on Mathematical Logic.

Dr. Warner has more than 15 years of experience in general math tutoring and tutoring for standardized tests such as the SAT, ACT and AP Calculus exams. He has tutored students both individually and in group settings.

In February 2010 Dr. Warner released his first SAT prep book "The 32 Most Effective SAT Math Strategies," and in 2012 founded Get 800 Test Prep. Since then Dr. Warner has written books for the SAT, ACT, SAT Math Subject Tests, AP Calculus exams, and GRE.

Dr. Steve Warner can be reached at

steve@SATPrepGet800.com

BOOKS BY DR. STEVE WARNER

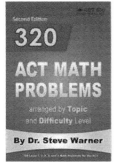

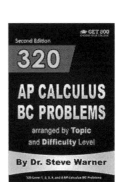

57611968R00113

Made in the USA
Middletown, DE
01 August 2019